HOW OWNE~~~, ~~~~~~~~~~

THAT'S IT

CAN MANUFACTURE

I'M FIRED

THEIR PRODUCT, SUCCESS, AND FREEDOM

THE
PUSH THRU

Website: www.thepushthru.com
Email: info@thepushthru.com
Phone: 918.371.7171
Address: 1810 N. 74th E Ave.
Tulsa, OK 74115

ISBN: 978-1-7379581-0-9 (print)
ISBN: 978-1-7379581-1-6 (ebook)

Ordering Information:
Special discounts are available on quantity purchases by corporations, associations, and others. For details, contact info@thepushthru.com or 918.371.7171

HOW OWNER/OPERATORS

THAT'S IT

CAN MANUFACTURE

I'M FIRED

THEIR PRODUCT, SUCCESS, AND FREEDOM

JEFF FINNEY

INTRODUCTION

IF YOU'RE A small-business owner who loves the thrill of being an entrepreneur but worries if all the long hours, days, weeks, months, years, and perhaps even decades will bring you the rewards you envisioned back when the entrepreneurial dream called you, then you've come to the right place.

This book will guide you through a set of principle-inspired steps, ranging from casting your vision to finally taking your hands off the metaphorical wheel and letting your carefully tuned enterprise drive itself. In other words, this book will help you learn how to *fire yourself* from the frenetic demands of owning and running your small business.

But don't worry—I won't ask you to sit back and watch your business operate like one of the many autonomous vehicles most drivers are still quite leery about. Although I'm a big fan of automation, businesses, like most cars, still require a human touch. However, as an exhausted small-business owner, you might be feeling that your business requires too much of your touch, and you need a break. Now is the time to learn what I finally did—that a business owner's ultimate goal should be to have a business that runs so efficiently he or she can step away from it with no worries.

If you're still trying to free yourself from the unceasing daily demands of your business, I know what you're feeling. Drained, right? As owner of Ultimate Cabinet Components (UCC) in Oklahoma, I spent years putting in those long hours, working my fingers almost literally to the bone. But I've learned some things since then that have made my life more enjoyable, and in this book, I'll share those things with you.

If you are or think you might be ready to make the move, then take your hands off the steering wheel for a few hours, trust your employees, and read on to learn how to *fire yourself*.

TABLE OF CONTENTS

CHAPTER 1

|————————————————————————|

FIRE YOURSELF

Don't forget until too late that the business of life is not
business but living.
—B. C. Forbes[1]

I NEVER IMAGINED I'd long to hear the words "You're fired." But seeing my business in dire straits despite my best efforts to pour myself wholeheartedly into a diminishing dream, I was pushing toward a place of despair, resigning myself to failure. Instead of me running the business, my business ruthlessly ran my life. Time with my family was scattered and short. Even my lunches were hurry-up affairs as I sought to return to the assembly line and work alongside my employees in meeting production quotas. All that stress and still I struggled to make a profit. Being fired really was beginning to sound like a good idea. But how does a boss fire himself?

That question was the epiphany that began the journey. Sometimes, even when you're the boss, you'll need to *fire yourself*.

Begin at the Beginning

Look back to when you started your business, and remember the reason you wanted to be your own boss. For most of us, it started with a desire to use our skills, make something out of nothing, and build a business we can be proud of. We wanted a business that provided a good living and the freedom from being a slave to our job, and the idea of creating something that could have significant value in the future to pass along to our children was too good to pass up.

But then somewhere along the way, reality smacked us in the face to remind us it's just not that easy. But why? When you're in a hurry to build the greatest business in the world, it's easy to forget to lay the foundation upon which a thriving company must be built. This begins with putting fundamentals in place that will ensure we have a company that works for us and not the other way around.

When I asked Martin Holland—my business coach, friend, and one of the nicest, most patient men I've ever met—about his most significant business failure, his reply surprised me. This agreeable, easygoing gentleman stated that his worst business failure occurred because of disagreements stemming from his and his business partner's lack of a shared vision and failure to define at the beginning what each of them wanted.

The vision you have is inescapably tied to your ultimate desire. Now, as a successful business coach, the first question Martin asks any new client is "What do you want?" Once your vision can be clearly defined, the first step in creating the foundation for your business can be taken.

Before we begin, I must reemphasize the importance of building the foundation first and not skipping any steps along the way. This book is a tactical guide for getting you, the business owner, into the position to work *on* your business and not just *in* it.

Let's start with a few housekeeping items (steps) you'll need to take care of to prepare your company for the changes about to take place.

STEP ONE: Follow Your Vision

Write down the vision for your business. Picture your vision as a lighthouse that's out of reach, far ahead in the distance. The lighthouse keeps you on the right path, toward safe harbor, and free of the rocky coastal shoals. Every decision you make from here on needs to be based on this vision. This step of casting and following your vision will be the focus of chapter two.

For now, my simple approach to staying true to your vision can be summed up with the word *no*. As hard as it is to say no, doing so is imperative to building the business of your dreams. You cannot be everything to everyone all the time. If you find yourself straying from the vision, just locate the lighthouse and get realigned. This simple practice has become almost second nature for my own business, and now my managers often refer to it to keep me in check. We'll examine this concept too in a bit more detail later on.

In 2018, I had the opportunity to expand my business by purchasing a struggling company. The products they offered were like ours but different enough that the buyout would have been a bit of a stretch. After a couple months of meetings and negotiations, my second-in-command asked me the simple question I'd failed to ask myself. "Does this buyout line up with where we're going?" The next day the deal was dead. Since then, as a team, we've doubled in size and are still growing because we followed the vision and focused on what we do well. And this true story leads directly to what you'll need to do next.

STEP TWO: Listen to the Opinions of Your Employees

The second item you need to address is your employees' opinions. Ask each of them what they'd do differently if they owned the business. Because the question is hypothetical, it encourages them to give honest answers. The hardest part of this exercise is biting your tongue and just listening. To start, simply field the answers and reflect on them as you move on to the next steps. I often continue to do this exercise on a random basis. Every employee knows that at any time I could ask them any one or more of the following questions:

- What would you do if you owned this company?

- What would make your job easier?

- What is your favorite thing about working here?

- What do you wish would change the most?

- What really bugs you?

The first time I ever asked these questions, I was taken aback at the honesty of the answers. Of course, a couple jokers said they'd give everyone raises (a topic we'll examine later). However, a few suggestions really made a quick impact. One employee said we should have more brooms because they could never find one when needed. That was an easy fix, and now we have brooms all over the shop. Another said there could be better communication, particularly as it related to individual tasks for the day. After getting some clarification, we figured out a way to use our current schedule to better convey responsibilities on the task lists.

Although those ideas were small, they had a lasting impact on the company because they focused on people rather than profits. It's my belief that in the end profits will always occur if the focus is on the customers and the team of employees we work with. Conversely, putting profits first tends to be a losing proposition.

My friend Bobby Lewis, CEO of Lewis Cabinet Specialties, correctly says, "At the end of the day, money doesn't matter. What matters is how many lives you've affected."[2] Bobby said this as the Lewis family's business grew and he came to a realization. "We were no longer in the business of manufacturing doors; we're now in the people business." For a business to truly succeed, that philosophy needs to permeate the company's culture from top to bottom and from CEO to custodian. If we work with the philosophy that we're here for each other, profits will take care of themselves.

By getting our employees in a frame of mind similar to our own, we encourage them to think like owners. Although not actual owners of the company, they will be more likely to take ownership for their function and responsibilities of their role in the company's success. Years ago, the Albertsons grocery chain had a catchy ad slogan that went like this: "It's Joe Albertson's supermarket, but the produce department is mine."[3] The message to shoppers was that the department managers took pride and had a sense of ownership in their departments.

The point here is that a grocery store or any other business in which the employees are fully invested emotionally will be run efficiently and can be trusted. What you, the owner, convey as important, employees will generally see as important too. If it's your goal to see continuous improvement in your company, then you need to be the poster child for that improvement, or you won't have any followers.

STEP THREE: The Organization Chart

The third step in this process is to prepare a simple organization chart. I know that for many this sounds silly, but it goes hand in hand with having a vision. You can find templates for this kind of chart online at Template.net, which I've found to be an outstanding resource. And since you're likely to be the only one who will use the chart, it doesn't need to be elaborate.

For the few who might be unaware of what an organization chart looks like, it's simply a series of boxes filled with job titles and the name of the person functioning in the role for that box. The boxes are connected by lines showing the relationship of each position to the others.

A typical organization chart looks something like this:

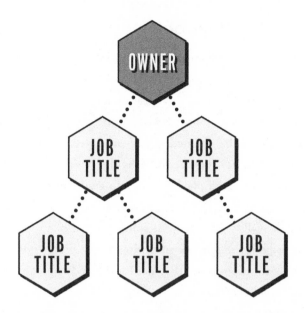

As you build your chart, don't hold back or allow limiting thoughts to discourage you from adding more boxes. When I initially wrote my chart, I had a hard time putting a box in for a chief financial officer (CFO), as I didn't believe I'd ever need a CFO. But the truth is I already had one. It was me!

When you build your chart, you'll begin to understand what this process of firing yourself entails. Even if you have to leave some or all of the boxes blank, make a job title for every position your ideal company would have. Only when you finish this step and know each of the job titles it takes to make your company run can you start plugging names into the boxes.

At first, you might be surprised by how many boxes your name is in. If you're anything like I was several years ago, then your name is probably in a majority of them. As I examined the chart, the solution to my business struggles was staring right back at me. I needed other names to replace mine in the boxes.

Probe the Playbook

In order to be successful at firing yourself, you must become relentless about creating a standard operating procedure (SOP). SOPs are the backbone of any great manufacturing business and convey the company standards in a way that's easy to understand. In fact, it should be required of your managers or supervisors to continually add and update SOPs as the business grows. Every successful coach has a playbook to help guide his or her players as they learn the team's values, processes, and successful plays. A company's SOPs serve a purpose similar to that of a sports team's playbook. So it shouldn't be surprising that SOPs are not a set-it-and-forget-it proposition. They need to be updated from time to time or completely redone depending on the circumstances. We'll focus more specifically on SOPs a little later in chapter three.

Pick One: Player or Coach

If you've come this far, you're on the road to firing yourself. Now it's time to look at your organization chart and find the one thing you're doing that's the greatest hinderance to the company's success. If you're in manufacturing I am, then I'll bet it's the shop floor that's holding you back. Although working on the shop floor is rewarding because you can see the results, it's also likely that you're best at selling and guiding your business. Think for a moment about how much more you could sell if you didn't have to constantly focus most of your energy on daily production.

Have you also ever noticed in your business that sales activity and cash flow seem to be mutually exclusive? In other words, when you're hitting the streets and drumming up new work, your cash flow decreases. Then, when you land some of that work and start production, the revenue rebounds, but your sales activity drops. As a business owner wearing several hats, it can often be difficult to navigate these times of feast or famine. More importantly, it can be hard to understand why it's happening.

I call this process *the vicious sales cycle,* and it occurs because when the owner is out selling, the manufacturing naturally declines as he or she is no longer driving the production and generating sufficient quantities of finished goods. However, a continual sales effort is necessary to maintain a sustainable business. If you aren't continually selling, then expect the ebb and flow of the sales/ cash cycle to happen repeatedly. And although this might sound odd at first, it's exactly why it's so important to work toward firing yourself.

A Frame of Mind

Throughout this book we're going to learn how to fire ourselves and develop the kind of business we set out to build from that very first day. Firing yourself is a frame of mind and is a philosophy that must be at the core of the business. If your employees understand that your goal as an owner is to have them run the production while you run the business, everyone wins.

Next, we'll discuss how to formulate and follow that lighthouse vision statement I mentioned briefly above that will be the first and likely most important step in the self-firing process.

CHAPTER CHECKLIST

1. Look back to when you started your business, and remember the reason you wanted to be your own boss.

2. Have you ever clearly defined what you want—the first step in developing your vision statement? If not, work to do so.

3. Write a formal vision statement. This will help you in several ways as you move forward.

4. Do you have the need for employee buy-in and realize its importance to your vision for the business? Begin to work and make this happen.

5. There's great value in preparing an organization chart. Will you do so?

6. Can you see the value in writing out a series of SOPs? It's never too early to get started with this step if you haven't already.

7. Do you see yourself as your team's coach or as one of the players? If you are one of the players, do you want to work toward becoming the coach?

8. If firing yourself has not been within your frame of mind, do you plan to revise your frame of mind?

ACTION ITEM: Look at your organization chart, and find the one thing you're doing that's the greatest hinderance to the company's success. If you don't have your organization chart, you must make one before moving forward. When you have your chart, find the one thing you're doing that's the greatest hinderance to the company's success. Do it now to avoid wasting untold hours and to start being more productive.

CHAPTER 2

LOOK TO YOUR LIGHTHOUSE

Once the lighthouse is seen, the rest of the sea is ignored.
—Terri Guillemets[4]

LIGHTHOUSES ARE, BECAUSE of their purpose, lonely places situated in remote, desolate, windswept areas. For many people, lighthouses stir up contemplative feelings. It's difficult to imagine what life in a lighthouse would be like. For those who have visited a lighthouse and seen the reality, few would want to stay for an extended period in such a secluded tower with little more than an endless expanse of violent, frothing waters stretching across the horizon. But were it not for lighthouses and the brave souls who operated them, countless lives and untold riches would have been lost to the ravages of violent coastal waters.

In the business world, tumult that's often as unsettling as 20-foot swells and bludgeoning breakers can be expected, and an entrepreneur can easily lose his or her way when facing financial shipwreck. The lighthouse can offer a clear vision statement, figuratively standing tall and unfazed by any raging storm, flashing its formidable beacon to all who seek safe passage into the safe harbor of a clear and constant purpose. As the experienced sailor or captain nears the coast's perilous shoreline, he stays steadfastly and singularly focused on the illuminating beam from the lighthouse, ignoring all else around him. Observing the roiling waves or the rocky coastline, while tempting, is courting disaster. After all, it's that lighthouse beacon alone that keeps the ship safely on course.

Your vision statement for your business is your lighthouse. Keep your eyes focused.

Lighting the Lamp

Over the centuries, a wide variety of systems have been used to illuminate the sky and warn vulnerable ocean-going vessels. The list includes fires, spider lamps, fountain lamps, mechanical overflow lamps, hydrostatic lamps, and many more. The point is none of the systems could be operated by simply flipping a switch, and they all required dedicated work to make illumination possible. And just as illuminating a lighthouse requires work, so too does developing a good vision statement. But doing so will pay huge dividends as you move forward.

Paige Arnof-Fenn, founder and CEO of the global strategic marketing consulting firm Mavens & Moguls, told journalist Sean Peek that "the vision should motivate the team to make a difference and be part of something bigger than themselves."[5] Moreover, research shows that employees who find their company's vision meaningful have engagement levels of 68 percent, which is 18 points above average.[6] In other words, a good vision statement will become an easily seen and appreciated lighthouse beacon, keeping more employees on track to the ultimate goal. On-track employees also mean a happier and more efficiently run company, which in turn translates into higher profits.

Randall Agee, founder and partner-owner of Allshore Virtual Staffing, began his career as a contracted computer programmer. When he found himself with more work than he could handle, he posted an ad on an international job board. The best applicant appeared to be one from Pakistan. Setting aside his hesitancy to take on the complications of international time zones and second languages, Randall connected with that applicant, and the two quickly recognized their connection. Rather than partnering for just that one project, the pair eventually formalized a partnership and founded Allshore Virtual Staffing—a company that now employs more than 120 people. With a common business vision, the pair has been able to clearly impart that same vision to their staffs within their five offices. I've seen the great results of this shared and established vision because my company is an Allshore Staffing client.

Just Say No

Before the vision for my company, UCC, was established, the business was what I'd label a *yes* company. This is because I was so focused on gaining clientele and maintaining a steady workflow that I took on almost any project offered to me—whether it was within my wheelhouse or not. But projects that can't be completed effectively, efficiently, and profitably are more a detriment than a benefit for any company. Saying no to a potential project can seem counterintuitive to a small-business owner trying to build a clientele, but sometimes no is yes.

As a rule, rejecting a project you're not able to complete effectively, efficiently, and profitably is always a smart business decision. All too often, saying yes without assessing whether a potential project aligns with your vision can lead you down an unprofitable path. In my view, a business owner must establish a vision and then reject any offers that stray from that vision.

At first glance it might seem easy to label that statement as unrealistic or too broad. Take my company's vision statement, for instance: *To be the most efficient cabinet component manufacturer in the world!* The hardest word for me to include in this statement was *world*. But after thinking about it for a while, I decided it was the only word that encompassed the way I felt about our business. I drew a clearly defined line in the sand even though I couldn't see exactly where the vision would end. To me, that's the key to crafting a great vision. It's easily understood and endlessly challenging.

For example, a ship's captain making his way to port through a brutal storm can't see the dock where he'll moor the ship but must faithfully follow the lighthouse beacon. Similarly, the business owner must understand that the vision's ultimate destination will likely remain just out of sight. You know it's out there, but it's obscured by the fog of life's complexities, and you must simply follow the vision's illumination relentlessly.

Don't be suckered into writing a weak vision statement that doesn't drive your company forward. If I were to have instead made my vision statement something like "the best cabinet component maker there is," it wouldn't have had the same effect. My actual statement is certainly grand, but it's also well defined. The latter is similar but too vague to be motivational. As stated, the vision instantly lets people know what the company is all about and drives my crew and me forward to meet the challenge of being "the most efficient cabinet component manufacturer in the world."

Do the same when crafting your company vision. Make it clear enough so that everyone understands it, but also ensure it's big enough that people around you will be motivated by it. What are your strong points as a business? What do you do well and why? What do you do poorly and why? Why did you want to start the company? Why does the company exist? Start looking for clues that help to tie your *whys* to your formal company vision. If you migrate toward the strong points of the business and tie them to your *whys*, then you're on your way to a strong vision. Keep it short and to the point but with big implications.

Here are a few vision statements, past and present, for you to study from some well-known companies:

- Disney: Make people happy.[7]

- IKEA: To create a better everyday life for the many people.[8]

- Microsoft: Empower every person and every organization on the planet to achieve more.[9]

- Nike: Crush Adidas.[10]

- Walmart: To "give customers a wide assortment of their favorite products, Every Day Low Prices, guaranteed satisfaction, friendly service, convenient hours, and a great online shopping experience."[11]

What do you like or dislike about each of those vision statements? Which one among them do you think would best serve as a lighthouse to guide huge corporate business decisions while still providing motivation for more mundane but still significant employee actions?

Think about the key elements you should take into account in developing your vision statement. Here are a few things I recommend considering to help get you started:

1. *It must honestly and accurately reflect your goal(s).* You must not take shortcuts. It's necessary that you know exactly where you want to go before getting underway. As a friend of mine often said, "If I aim for the wrong goal, success is the ultimate failure."

2. *It must be clear.* If your partners and/or employees can't understand the statement, it's useless. This is why you'll want to involve others in the process of developing it.

3. *It must be concise.* If you and your employees can't remember it, no one is likely to abide by it. Which of the vision statements listed above are most memorable to you? Most of the time, it's the shorter ones.

4. *It must be inspiring.* A lighthouse beacon that fails to reach mariners is of no value. A proper vision statement should prompt your employees to want what you want and be for the benefit of all.

5. *It must be continuously challenging.* There's no point in continuing past accomplished goals.

While there are others that could be added to this list, these five elements should be sufficient to keep you on course as you begin to write your vision statement. Once the vision statement is formally adopted, you can move on to the next crucial phase.

Lead, Follow, or Get Out of the Way

Founder and CEO of The SajiGroup and success coach Saji Ijiyemi says that "you are either supporting the vision or supporting division."[12] When the company's vision has been cast, accepted, and established as the guiding light, everyone within the company must support it and base their decisions and actions on their adherence to that vision. Anything short of that careful adherence will bring division, which can easily and quickly lead to collapse.

In 1988, the San Francisco 49ers drafted a supremely talented linebacker named William (Bill) Romanowski.[13] Romanowski played for several different teams throughout his 16-season-long NFL career and was chosen twice to play in the prestigious Pro Bowl. No one ever doubted Romanowski's talent. But his many altercations with teammates and opposing players caused many to question his commitment to the team. The sports network ESPN once listed Romanowski as the fifth dirtiest player in the history of team sports.[14]

I once had an employee who, though nowhere near as troublesome as Bill Romanowski, gave me an up-close-and-personal lesson in the problems a me-first employee can bring to a business. Wayne performed admirably the tasks he was hired to do, and because he'd performed so well, I gave him opportunities to take on expanded duties. However, each time I gave him an opportunity to advance, he proved to be unequal to the task. So, I reassigned him to his original job, where again he performed admirably. That should have been where things settled.

But Wayne watched and grew bitter as many of his colleagues—his teammates—advanced to higher positions. What he failed to realize was that I'd given him those same advancement opportunities and he'd underperformed. Yet despite those opportunities, Wayne's bitterness grew and eventually became more obvious to those around him. Since this had the potential to create wider dissension among the team members, I spoke with Wayne about his resentment, but still nothing changed. Everything about Wayne's attitude and his consequent efforts to embitter his teammates ran counter to our vision statement. So, for the good of the team and the company, I did what I knew I had to do—I fired him.

As I've said before, it's crucial that your employees share the vision. This means that as you brainstorm your vision statement, you should recall conversations with your employees and consider what motivates them to strive for their best—and, conversely, what discourages them. You might also consider recruiting a few of them to help you in these brainstorming sessions or provide them a questionnaire to fill out. A good questionnaire might include these questions:

- What is the most important thing this company is doing right?

- What is the most important thing this company could do better?

- What motivates you to do your best work?

- What within the current working environment discourages or frustrates you?

The answers to these questions can help to guide your vision statement–development process. Keep in mind that even the best businesses will have employee turnover, and this will be an ongoing challenge. As you hire either to replace departed employees or to expand operations, it's crucial to add employees who buy into your vision.

My Parkinson's Provocation

In 2017, the vision for my business and life suddenly became sharper and more focused when my doctor confirmed that the persistent tremors I was experiencing were the result of Parkinson's disease. He told me that it was likely that within 10 years I'd no longer be able to run my business—at least not to the level of involvement that had underscored my previous decade. That diagnosis accentuated and accelerated my need to pursue a vision of making UCC the most efficient cabinet component manufacturer in the world. I needed to realize my ultimate goal of firing myself so that I could follow B. C. Forbes's adage: "Don't forget until too late that the business of life is not business but living."[15]

CHAPTER CHECKLIST

1. Begin to formulate your plan for writing your vision statement. Try your best to include employee input in the procedure.

2. Define the *whys* that will drive the formulation of the vision statement. Write these down.

3. Evaluate other companies' vision statements to help you in formulating your own.

4. Give some thought to the five points in my list for formulating your vision statement.

5. Consider what might be the most effective method for involving your employees in developing the vision statement.

ACTION ITEM: If your company does not have a vision statement, focus on getting that started as soon as possible. If you do have one, review it and determine whether it truly charts the course you intend to follow. If not, begin revising or rewriting it.

CHAPTER 3

LOOK TO YOUR LESSONS LEARNED

Quality involves living the message of the possibility of
perfection and infinite improvement, living it day in and
day out, decade by decade.
—Tom Peters

IF YOUR AIM is to fire yourself, then your business needs to be able to hum along in your absence. Firing yourself doesn't mean abandoning your company. Instead, it means having the calm confidence that you can take your family on a weeks-long vacation and return to find your company thriving, your employees pursuing the vision, and, most importantly, your customers remaining loyal purchasers of your products or services.

This level of confidence takes time to develop, and it certainly requires a solid, dedicated team. But before we look at the concept and various elements of team building and teamwork, let's take some time to consider a key tool for building and empowering a team that will indeed give you the freedom to fire yourself. That key tool is your collection of standard operating procedures (SOPs).

Avoid Being an SOB by Scripting SOPs

SOPs are the backbone of any successful manufacturing business. They convey the company's standards in a way that's easily accessible and simple to understand. Most readers likely have at least an elementary concept of what an SOP is, but for those who don't, it can be defined as "established or prescribed methods to be followed routinely for the performance of designated operations or in designated situations."[16] In other words, SOPs should address in detail how a given task should be performed by providing a set of step-by-step instructions for any and every given task. SOPs allow you, the owner, to be free of the burden of having to constantly answer employees' questions about work procedures. All these interruptions are likely to turn you into a frustrated and impatient SOB. *To avoid becoming an SOB, create your SOPs.*

At UCC, we've set eight steps as the maximum number for any SOP. If a procedure requires more than eight steps, we break it into two or more SOPs. Remember the importance of keeping things short and simple. If you have a hard time with this, you can use my typical process for creating an easy-to-follow SOP. First, break down each step of the process, then snap a picture of what you are breaking down. For example, if the first step is turning the machine power on, then snap a picture of the main switch turned to the on position. Then, when the picture is put on paper, you add a simple caption that can be something like "turn main power *on*." Don't go into meticulous detail, and allow employees to employ their common sense to follow the basics. Next, laminate the SOPs for protection, place them on a key ring, and hang them right next to the station where that procedure takes place.

Recently, I saw one of my production workers pick up the SOP before performing a task she hadn't done in a while. She spent about half a minute reading it and then proceeded to perform the task as if she did so on a regular basis. She was able to do this because the SOP was comprehensive and concise. When I wrote my first few SOPs, they tended to be longer and required more reading, which meant employees were less likely to refer to them. Again, simplicity is essential. Now having seen firsthand the value of SOPs, my foremen and managers often create their own SOPs for their areas.

The Standard for Standardizing

Obviously not everything your employees do needs a written procedural standard. You likely don't need to post an SOP in your breakroom detailing how to warm lunch in the microwave. And unless you're operating a food-related business, you probably don't need to provide a step-by-step hand-washing SOP. But, on the other hand, we're mistaken if we assume that every task is sufficiently intuitive that employees can always figure them out on their own. The bottom line is to assume that any business-related procedure that's not commonly performed in everyday life should be explained in an SOP.

A Supreme SOP: Specific yet Simple

If you need an example of what an SOP should look like, here's one I wrote for changing a flat tire.

1. Find a safe place to perform the procedure, and prepare the car. Find a flat, level surface to change your flat. Turn off the ignition, and make sure the transmission is in park, or if it's a manual transmission, make sure it's not in neutral.

2. Get your spare tire, lug wrench, and jack (typically found under a lid at the bottom of the trunk) and use the lug wrench to *loosen* the lug nuts (turn counterclockwise but not too much).

3. Place the jack saddle directly under a flat portion of the car's frame near the flat tire. Jack up the car either by pumping (for a hydraulic jack) or by turning the jack handle clockwise (for a scissor jack). Raise the car high enough to remove the flat tire.

4. Use the lug wrench to finish removing the previously loosened lug nuts, and carefully pull the flat tire and wheel from the hub. Set it aside. Keep the lug nuts nearby in a spot where they can be easily retrieved.

5. Lift the spare, and align the holes in the wheels with the bolts on the hub as you slide the wheel of the spare into place. Tighten them *a bit* more with the lug wrench.

6. Lower the car by loosening the jack tension. You can do this by twisting the lock counterclockwise on a hydraulic jack or by turning the jack handle counterclockwise on a scissor jack.

7. Use the lug wrench to complete the tightening of the lug nuts.

If you'd never changed a tire, would the instructions (the SOP) above be sufficient to guide you through the procedure safely and efficiently? Was it detailed yet simple? Can you think of ways to improve this SOP? Now think of a procedure performed regularly in your production process and write out an SOP for that process.

SOPs in the Algorithmic Age

Your SOPs don't have to be in traditional written form like the tire-changing instructions above. In fact, in our fast-paced age of reduced or impatient attention spans, videos can often be a more effective method for recording and presenting SOPs. At UCC, we often film or audio record our regularly performed procedures and narrate the steps to provide visual instruction.

For example, when the company receives a new machine, we record the entire installation as a training session with a lavalier microphone on the installer to get 720p digital audio. I then send the raw footage to a local photographer to edit the videos into smaller instructional clips (approximately five minutes) by topic. This allows employees to watch the training videos here at our facilities or remotely by uploading the videos to YouTube.

When SOPs Solve Spats and Streamline Systems

A spat between two of my good, most conscientious employees led to a significant procedural production modification. One of the workers was unsatisfied with the work done by his colleague who preceded him in the production process. Their argument produced no results, and they went their separate ways with the second worker adjusting the work of his predecessor on that particular piece. However, that response was only a short-term fix for a bigger issue.

When I heard about the incident, I called for a company-wide meeting. I assigned no blame to either employee. Instead, I led the team in a discussion aimed at finding and resolving the root problem. The result was a more productive process in that phase. Then, at that same meeting, I opened the floor for every employee to bring up similar issues. In that one meeting, we identified and corrected at least 10 nagging issues that had hindered unity and production. Some of those solutions required writing new SOPs.

Don't Worry; Be Bendy

In order to survive and thrive, your business needs to grow and adapt to cultural changes and industry innovations that influence customers' purchasing decisions. That means that your SOPs cannot remain static and will need to be updated periodically. When cultural changes or industry innovations start to affect your financial bottom line, don't worry. Instead, be bendy and flexible.

This will ensure you're not left behind. A procedure might have been the best practice for decades, but when new technology provides a more efficient and cost-effective procedure, don't be mired in the muck of monotony. Always move on and adapt when possible.

As the lighthouse technology listed in chapter two progressed from simple fires to more sophisticated and efficient illuminating systems, the lighthouse operators had to upgrade the systems, knowledge of the systems, and SOPs for managing and maintaining the systems. Another step in the process of firing yourself is to be ready to update your SOPs as needed.

SOP TEMPLATE

#1 Open Card with COD Sticker	#2 Verify deposit amount on Master Sales Commission Form	#3 Open invoice in project quoter—if necessary, update, overwrite, and save as final pdf.	#4 Find invoice in Dropbox and attach to drawing on shop floor.
#5 Call customer and email final invoice.			

CHAPTER CHECKLIST

1. If you've not already done so, write one or more SOPs for your business. If you're not confident that they serve their purpose, revise them as needed.

2. Determine what other procedures within your business would be made more efficient if written into an SOP.

3. As you think through your roster of employees, can you imagine them appreciating or disliking a set of SOPs? Change any SOPs you're unsure of.

4. As you consider the task of writing SOPs, determine if you're best suited to write them or if you should seek assistance instead.

5. If you like the idea of audiovisual SOPs, do you have the means to make them? Are you willing to invest enough money to make reasonably high-quality SOP videos? These are all factors to consider before you begin to create them.

6. Are you building a "bendy" business, one that is flexible enough to adapt to cultural changes and industry advancements?

ACTION ITEM: Take a look at one of the SOPs you've written. How did it turn out? Was it comprehensive but still concise? If not, keep working on it.

CHAPTER 4

|————————————————————————|

TWO-CHECK TUESDAYS OR TRIUMPHANT TEAMWORK?

Talent wins games, but teamwork and
intelligence win championships.
—Michael Jordan[17]

MICHAEL JORDAN PLAYED his last NBA game on April 16, 2003, nearly two decades ago.[18] But even with the passage of time, one would be hard pressed to find any American who has not at least heard the name Michael Jordan, very probably the greatest basketball player of all time. Yes, despite the remarkable skills of more recent stars like LeBron James and Steph Curry, most basketball pundits and die-hard NBA fans still rate Michael Jordan as the greatest of all time, or the GOAT.[19, 20] His basketball exploits are legendary and include 10 individual scoring titles.[21] Yet it was he who famously said, "Talent wins games, but teamwork and intelligence win championships."[22]

The very best teams that win championships are composed of dedicated and talented—but not necessarily all-star level—individuals who are able to mesh as a cohesive unit. The 1969 New York Mets had an up-and-coming star pitcher named Tom Seaver but otherwise had an average roster. When that Mets team surprisingly made it all the way to the World Series, they faced a Baltimore Orioles superteam, stacked with megastars that included Dave McNally, Jim Palmer, Boog Powell, Brooks Robinson, and Frank Robinson.[23] After winning 109 regular-season games,[24] the Orioles were heavily favored to win the Series, but it was the Mets' teamwork that was able to overcome the Orioles' star power to win baseball's most prestigious prize.

My Baseball Experience: Talent versus Teamwork

I saw and was intimately part of similar situations during my teen years. Despite living in a part of the country where football was the dominant sport, I fell in love with baseball. And because of my dedication to the game, I became proficient at both batting and fielding. However, the little town I lived in had few other young men with similar enthusiasm and consequential skills for the game. Following my sophomore year when the coaches of the American Legion team from nearby Dewey, Oklahoma, invited me to join their team, the Bulldoggers, I was on cloud nine.

The talent level on the Bulldoggers team was light-years ahead of the team I'd been on the year before. We began to win games and make a name for ourselves. But this ended up being too good to be true. Midway through the season, the team began to disintegrate into bickering individuals. It wasn't long before some of my teammates revolted against the head coach, who eventually stepped aside and was replaced by his assistant. Though our roster remained unchanged with plenty of talented individuals, our team wins became less frequent. We declined from a juggernaut in the early season to a team that missed the playoffs.

The following summer, after a great season as a junior in high school, a friend and I made the cut for a super-talented Bartlesville team. But a bureaucratic technicality sent us back to Dewey. The individual talent level on that year's Dewey team was no match for the talent on the Bartlesville team, but the new Dewey coach developed a team culture unlike anything I'd ever experienced. Despite our average individual talent, we won a regional championship, and I learned a not-to-be-forgotten lesson about teamwork and the importance of coaching.

Draft the Best "Athletes"—Regardless of Position

Even the best coach can't win consistently without at least a few superstar players. However, it isn't always easy to see into the future and pick the best possible athlete—or, for business bosses, to hire the best work applicant. What complicates this process further is that an applicant's experience may not always be the best means for forecasting success. Sometimes, choosing the right job applicant is as difficult for a business owner as choosing the right roster additions for a pro sports coaching staff. An example of this can be seen in the 2000 NFL draft. That year, 198 college players were selected ahead of Tom Brady,[25] who, with seven Super Bowl championships and a myriad of records, is now widely regarded as the greatest quarterback in NFL football history.[26] Like the New England Patriots scouting team, business recruiters need to watch carefully for less noticed diamonds in the rough who might just go on to be MVPs in the future.

On the other hand, sometimes business owners make the kind of mistake the NBA's Portland Trailblazers have made not once but twice. In the 1984 draft, the Blazers assumed their greatest need was at the center position, so they selected the 7'1" Sam Bowie with the number two pick. This allowed the Chicago Bulls to choose Michael Jordan, the GOAT mentioned above, at number three. Sam Bowie went on to have an average but injury-shortened NBA career, while Michael Jordan led the Bulls to six championships.[27]

Twenty-three years after missing out on Michael Jordan, the Blazers again perceived their greatest need to be at the center position, selecting 7'0" Greg Oden. Like Sam Bowie, Oden had an average but injury-shortened NBA career. The Blazers' second big mistake gave the Seattle Supersonics the opportunity to select Kevin Durant with the league's number two pick. Today, Durant is widely considered to be one of the top 10 NBA players of all time.[28]

If I have a choice between one applicant with more experience and another who has less experience but a more trainable attitude and better overall aptitudes, I'll always choose attitude and aptitude over specific experience. In other words, I'll select the candidate who is, figuratively, the best athlete rather than making the kind of big mistake the Portland Trailblazers made twice.

Two-Check Tuesdays and the Flynn Phenomenon

Another way of looking at the concept of high-level hiring versus everyday-expedience hiring is through what's referred to in the construction industry as "two-check Tuesdays." Fired or laid-off employees generally get two paychecks—one from the previous week and another for the current week's pay up to the point of termination. I always hated two-check Tuesdays, primarily because I dislike letting employees go.

Sure, at times it's necessary to replace employees. The bad ones must go immediately, or they can wreck an organization. The mistake often comes at the very beginning. When we hastily hire any applicant—or, as I sometimes refer to it, "hiring a heartbeat"—to fill an opening, we set ourselves up for failure. Hiring an employee needs to be strategic and deliberate to avoid costly training expenses and rapid employee turnover that can destroy a company.

Another example from the sports world of how this rush to fill an opening went wrong can be seen in the 2011 NFL season. Matt Flynn, Aaron Rodgers's backup quarterback in Green Bay, was given a three-year, $19 million contract by the Seattle Seahawks based on one successful end-of-the-season game for the Packers. During that same off-season, the Seahawks selected a somewhat-obscure quarterback from Wisconsin named Russell Wilson.[29] Wilson outperformed Flynn at their training camp and was named the team's starter. Wilson led his team to a win in Super Bowl 48 and became a megastar, while Flynn faded into the shadows.[30] Despite Flynn's lack of performance, he kept that eight million while he sat on the sidelines. This turned out to be a terrible investment for the Seahawks.

Keep in mind too of the high costs associated with employee turnover. In a recent article on the Balance Careers website, it was pointed out that "employee turnover carries a high cost and the higher the employee turnover rate, the higher the cost. Smart companies work hard to measure employee satisfaction and act to minimize turnover. It's cheaper to keep your current employees motivated and productive than it is to find, hire, and train new ones."[31]

Here are a few figures gathered by Terra Staffing Group:

- It costs $12,000 to replace an entry-level employee making $36,000 a year.

- It costs $20,000 to replace a manager making $60,000 a year.

- It costs $50,000 to replace an executive making $150,000 a year.[32]

Résumés as Scouting Reports

Pro sports teams typically have scouting teams that spend countless hours attending college games and watching game tapes to evaluate potential recruits' chances of success. The scouts' goal is to find those future stars like Tom Brady, Russell Wilson, and Michael Jordan. As draft day approaches, team officials pore over their scouts' player evaluations. The process is still something of a guessing game, but the guesses are at least guided by experienced assessments of a player's strengths and weaknesses.

As a business owner, selecting finalists for interviews based on their application forms and résumés can be a daunting experience. From my experience, here's what I'd suggest you look for as you peruse the piles of résumés from would-be team members:

1. *Presentation*: Does the applicant's résumé reveal clear thinking and suitable organizational skills? Even though your opening might be for a mechanic and not an editor, a mechanic who lacks the care to present himself well in his résumé likely might not be the best at paying attention to detail when he replaces those brake pads and calipers or flushes a radiator.

2. *Endurance*: Does the applicant's work history reveal a lack of stability? If the applicant has a history of short stays at previous places of employment, there's a good chance that he or she lacks stability and perseverance—two qualities that are prominent among top-level employees.

3. *Measurable performance*: Does the applicant's résumé cite specific examples of accomplishments? Vague references to successes could be signs of a lack of industriousness. It might also reveal a tendency to attempt deception.

4. *General experience*: Remember, specific experience is not the end-all in applicant selection. As I wrote above, I generally rate a trainable attitude at least as highly as specific experience. Training and coaching job-specific duties is easier than instilling a proper attitude and a genuine desire to take on responsibilities.

5. *Positive referrals*: I've found that, as a rule and within legal regulations, former employers go out of their way

to provide accurate and beneficial evaluations of former employees. If the candidate gets a glowing review from former employers, he or she is likely to be a great asset for your business.

Tryouts: The Interview

Early on in my business, I was the ultimate micromanager. After all, I knew better than anyone what I wanted. So why trust that goal to anyone else? Because tied to that method is the view that employees are little more than robots with buttons to push to perform rote functions. And tied to that view is the notion that employers should maximize profits by minimizing compensation. The problem with that line of thinking is that it leads to high turnover. And as detailed above, retaining good employees is more cost effective than constantly hiring new employees. This is one of the big reasons why I completely changed my hiring process.

After posting an opening on sites like Craigslist, my managers and I hold office interviews to cull the number of applicants down to three or four. Then we bring in each of those finalists for a few full-day, working interviews. At the end of each day, we pay them as contract workers. For evaluation, we ask the employees the recruit worked with that day to detail the recruit's performance. For this, a simple evaluation questionnaire will suffice. End the survey with this question: Could you picture yourself working long term with the recruit? This method completely changed our turnaround and increased our probability of landing a great employee. It can do the same for your company too.

Since the internet is loaded with sites offering interview advice and even specific questions to ask, I'll just reemphasize that doing the hard work of finding, hiring, and retaining high-quality employees up front saves time and money in the long run. Take a long-term approach and think strategically. When you find the right people, bite the bullet and spend as necessary to get and keep high-quality employees. In the long term, you'll save money and create fewer headaches.

You've Found Them; Now Can You Keep Them?

For decades, professional athletes were treated as indentured servants. Teams drafted players and then determined their salaries. The players had no say in what team they played for or how much they were paid. During the late '60s and early '70s, one Major League Baseball player, Curt Flood, agitated for a change in those conditions. Though Curt Flood never got his wish to choose the team he'd like to play for, by late 1975, pro athletes won their right to do as Curt Flood had called for.[33] They became free agents and could work for whomever they chose.

Think of your employees and prospective employees as free agents. In most cases, they can, at any time, leave your company and go somewhere else. In some cases, this can be a good thing, and you might even find yourself muttering, "Don't let the door hit you on the way out." But what about those valuable employees, the ones who show up on time every day and perform their duties efficiently and profitably? The ones who go above and beyond because of their outstanding work ethic. What are you willing to do to keep them?

Each of the steps listed above could be potentially costly and time consuming. But each can also be effective for employee retention.

Remember to always look back at the high cost of employee turnover and think long term. If you can pick the right employees up front, your business has a much higher chance at retaining them for the long haul. Strive for a business that employees never want to leave, and potential candidates are knocking down the door to become the newest member.

Employee Retention Resources

- *Orientation*: A new employee who must figure out for themself the company culture, the specifics of the job responsibilities, and all the procedures will quickly become discouraged and tempted to go elsewhere. Investing in new-employee orientation is a worthwhile expenditure. I found this article, "How to Create an Effective New Employee Orientation Program," on Indeed.com to be a worthwhile resource.[34]

- *Competitive compensation*: You must pay your employees competitive salaries and benefits if you want to keep them. For more assistance, read the article "What's in a Comprehensive Employee Benefits Package?" by Susan M. Heathfield.[35]

  - » Note: Compensation can come in forms other than just higher salaries or higher hourly rates. Consider the following:

  - » Work with other businesses to offer your employees discounted products and services on things like office supplies, automotive repairs, plumbing services, landscape services, and health club memberships.

» Offer monthly or weekly performance rewards programs.

» Include a weekly or monthly free lunch.

» Provide a prime parking space for the employee of the month.

» Give away free passes to a movie or to a pro sports game.

- *Ongoing training*: A well-trained employee is more likely to be a productive and contented employee.

- *Good communication*: An employee who understands company objectives and expectations is more likely to be a productive and contented employee. For more assistance on company communication, check out the article "5 Proven Ways to Improve Your Company's Communication" by Murray Newlands.[36]

- *Performance reviews*: Employees need to know what they're doing well and where they need to improve. And, of course, pay raises should be tied to good performance. For more assistance on performance reviews, see this article, "10 Key Tips for Effective Employment Reviews," by Susan M. Heathfield for help.

- *Positive work environment*: Employees who are free from harassment, who feel they are part of a dedicated and valued team, and who feel respected are more likely to perform at high levels. For more assistance on creating a positive work environment read the article "Top 10 Ways to Create a Positive Work Environment" by Ahmad Emarah.[37]

CHAPTER CHECKLIST

1. Have you ever calculated your annual percentage of employee turnover? If not, and if you'd like to do so, according to Indeed.com, this is how to do it:

   » Determine how many employees left in each month as well as the average number of employees your company had in the same month.

   » Divide the average number of employees by the number of employees who left in the month being analyzed.

   » Multiply this number by 100.[38]

2. Have you ever calculated your annual costs for employee turnover? If not, plan to start.

3. Do you agree that spending more time and resources in recruiting and keeping high-quality employees is a better investment than paying the costs of employee churn? If so, give this business strategy a try.

4. What types of creative compensation would you be inclined to offer in order to retain top-notch employees? Make a list and determine what you're able to offer.

ACTION ITEM: Do a little research. What are other employers with similar businesses in your area paying their employees? How does your pay scale and compensation package compare? If you're well below the average, bite the bullet and begin to pay competitive wages.

CHAPTER 5

GIVING LEAN VELOCITY

*LEAN has to be a culture, not something
employees are forced to do.*
—Jeff Finney

I INTERVIEWED PAUL Akers, author of the *2 Second
LEAN*, and owner of FastCap, in 2018. This book transformed
my thinking, so I had to have the author on my *Push Thru*
podcast. If you're like me, the first time you meet Paul Akers, you
start to question your effectiveness in not only your work but in
your life more generally. Fast-paced is an understatement when
used to describe Paul's lifestyle. He's a person who just gets things
done, and my interview with Paul was only able to scrape the
surface of LEAN manufacturing. Every piece of advice from Paul
is something you can use today to begin improving your business,
health, and life as a whole.

Paul's success with LEAN is something he attributes to his passion, curiosity, and approach to every situation with the mindset of "let's see what happens." Be relentless with *what-if* questions, he says, and never shy away from opportunities. His advice to all business owners is to become "passionate hillbillies" who stay humble in all circumstances.[39] Make it a point to find out what happens if you make a change or try a new method, and don't settle for where you are today.

What Is LEAN?

In general terms, here's what the LEAN Enterprise Institute stands for:

> A lean organization understands customer value and focuses its key processes to continuously increase it. The ultimate goal is to provide perfect value to the customer through a perfect value creation process that has zero waste.

> To accomplish this, lean thinking changes the focus of management from optimizing separate technologies, assets, and vertical departments to optimizing the flow of products and services through entire value streams that flow horizontally across technologies, assets, and departments to customers.[40]

More specifically, the basic premise of Paul Akers's *2 Second LEAN* is that if you make a two-second improvement each day, the cumulative result will end up making a big impact.[41] LEAN is about eliminating waste through continual improvement and through growing people. Two seconds is an amount of time I think we can all handle.

The key to Paul's version of LEAN is that he doesn't set out to improve the bottom line. Instead, he uses it to improve his life. By making a two-second improvement every single day, he finds his life to be easier and more productive—things that most of us stive for.

The three steps of *2 Second LEAN* are *sweep*, *sort*, and *standardize*.[42]

STEP ONE: Sweep

This is as simple as it sounds. But what caught my attention is how it's implemented at FastCap. Every single morning, they follow the three steps of *2 Second LEAN* and start by literally sweeping and getting rid of any unneeded clutter or trash.

I've always tried to have my employees sweep at the end of every day. Some do it, and some don't. I see now that doing it at the beginning of the day makes sense because employees have more energy before starting their daily tasks. On the other hand, at the end of the day everyone is ready to go home, and cleaning can be put on the back burner.

STEP TWO: Sort

Immediately after sweeping, employees will sort their areas. If there are tools or products that don't belong in that area, they're put back in their place. This is the step that people are most likely to overlook. Think about it. How often have you looked for a Phillips screwdriver only to find a hundred flat screwdrivers?

Sorting an area daily ensures that everything is in its place and can easily be found when needed. My company recently began to use

Kaizen foam from FastCap to sort tools at each station so that if there's an empty hole in the foam, there's clearly a tool missing.

STEP THREE: Standardize

To summarize, standardizing makes cross-training possible, controls quality, and establishes universal benchmarks for everyone to follow. As we saw in chapter three, SOPs are a key element in standardizing.

The Pillars of Improvement

As a company, we guide all our improvements with these three pillars:

1. Continually improve.

2. Eliminate waste.

3. Create value for our customers.

More succinctly, we often say in our morning stand-up meetings that *we create value for our customers by eliminating waste through continuous improvement.*

Pillar 1: Continually Improve

Continuous improvement might sound easy, and at the core, it really is. The difficulty is that in practice it can often be hard to sustain. One way to continuously strive to improve is to *always* have a morning meeting. You can make the agenda whatever you like, but meet *every* morning. We start at seven a.m. with our three steps (sweep, sort, and standardize) for 30 minutes and follow this with our meeting, which is about 10 to 15 minutes long. This meeting is when we talk about LEAN concepts, improvement, and any changes that need to be made.

One of my favorite morning topics to discuss is work presentation. Recently, we've started to shift our thinking inside the shop. Here's an example. The CNC machine operator looks at the edge-bander operator as their customer, the bander looks to the dowel machine, the dowel machine looks to the sorter, and so on.

I came to the realization that so often in our shop our individual tasks are looked at as our only job. However, if we look at the next person in the line as our customer, then we might be motivated to go the extra mile to make their job easier. What if the operator can present their work in such a manner that makes the next person's job easier? This led to a conversation that hadn't taken place before and is where I believe we will see the biggest payoff of the LEAN concept.

Pillar 2: Eliminate Waste

Eliminating waste is where my brain goes on tilt. Every time I walk through the shop, all I see is waste. It's absolutely everywhere. We have made more than 100 improvements, but there is still waste everywhere we look. When we first started continuous improvement, waste was easy to spot, like low-hanging fruit. Now that we have taken care of the easy stuff, we have to look harder to find waste in the system. That said, if we continue to peel back the layers, we always find more waste. Currently at UCC, we are focused on wasted motion and how many "touches" we have on a product or part.

The effect on our shop so far has been amazing. Now we're producing about 20 percent more work with one less person, and we still have room to get better. I spend a lot of time on the shop floor looking at our processes and figuring out better ways to do things. What I've noticed is that employees are getting more into LEAN because they see how it makes their lives easier. When each person took an honest look at his or her part of the shop and fixed what bugged them, a lot of our problems with waste were solved.

Pillar 3: Creating Value for the Customer

The great thing about eliminating waste and continuously striving to improve is that it ultimately provides the customer with more value. Customers don't pay us to carry boards around, ship incomplete orders, or have unused talent in the shop. They pay us for a complete, well-built product that is on time and cost efficient. This is what drives me personally to adopt the LEAN concepts in our shop. I want our customers to love our products and never question that they're receiving great value.

Making LEAN Last

Most of the time when I walk through the shop, I can find several ways to easily reduce waste. From too many steps to overprocessing, there's time wasted, and I know my company needs more LEAN. The problem is deciding to begin a LEAN initiative and sticking to it. What often happens is that we implement new systems and practices, and over time, they fizzle out. Figuring out why this happens is an important step.

I believe the answer starts at the top. If the owner or CEO doesn't live it, then why would everyone else in the operation? I now understand that if I, the owner, approach LEAN from a philosophical perspective, implementing it will be much easier. LEAN has to be a culture, not something employees are forced to do.

Along those lines, it's important to remember that you hired your production employees to work the production processes, not to streamline the administrative processes. That's the job of the owners and administrators. For example, requiring employees to set aside their normal duties to record in and out times (job on, job off) for certain processes is essentially assigning administrative tasks to people who weren't hired to do administrative tasks. Such diversions can reduce rather than improve customer value.

LEAN manufacturing isn't primarily about cutting costs by reducing the workforce. Again, the purpose of these evaluations is to streamline processes, which in turn builds efficiency. This saves the business owner, employees, and, yes, the customers time and money. One of my mottos is "We are creating value for our customers through continuously improving procedures and eliminating waste." And, as you might remember, my company's vision statement is "To be the most efficient cabinet component manufacturer in the world!"

CHAPTER CHECKLIST

1. If, as the Lean Enterprise Institute says, "the ultimate goal [of LEAN] is to provide perfect value to the customer through a perfect value creation process that has zero waste,"[43] then what is your company doing to eliminate waste? If you can't answer that question, begin to look at ways you can work to eliminate waste.

2. Sweeping, the first step in the *2 Second LEAN*, can be literal and metaphorical. If, in your situation, it is literal, do your employees have all the right tools to make a fast, effective sweep of the shop floor? If, for you, it's metaphorical, explain what it means to you and how you can improve the sweeping process.

3. Do you agree that having daily morning meetings is an efficient use of time and a key to continuous improvement? If so, explain how it helps. If not, give your reasons.

4. A LEAN culture starts at the top. How are you making your daily use of time more LEAN?

ACTION ITEM: Pick one small thing, right now, that can make a two-second improvement in your use of time and state how you'll implement it.

CHAPTER 6

AUTOMATE THE ANTIQUATED

*Rather than wringing our hands about robots taking over
the world, smart organizations will embrace strategic
automation use cases. Strategic decisions will be based on
how the technology will free up time to do the types of tasks
that humans are uniquely positioned to perform.*
—Clara Shih[44]

THROUGHOUT HUMANITY'S EXISTENCE,
prophets of doom have warned of the grave dangers of technological
advancements and automation. For example, just recently Mark
Cuban, the billionaire owner of the NBA's Dallas Mavericks and
star of the TV show *Shark Tank*, declared, "Automation is going to
cause unemployment, and we need to prepare for it."[45]

Is this true? Does automation cause unemployment? Well, yes, certainly automation can cause short-term, localized unemployment in the specific area in which a machine or a computer program replaces humans. Henry Ford's automation of automobile production put thousands of carriage makers and crossing sweepers—the brave souls who daily worked in deplorable conditions to remove the millions of tons of horse manure that soiled city streets throughout the nation—out of work.

According to an article on the website World History, "in 1918, only one in 13 families owned a car. By 1929, four out of five families had one. In the same time period, the number of cars on the road increased from eight million to 23 million. In fact, the industry grew so fast, by 1925 over 10% of all people in the workforce had something to do with production, sales, service, or fueling of automobiles."[46] Automated production of automobiles put millions of Americans to work and removed countless tons of putrid horse manure. The loss of a few thousand carriage makers' and manure movers' jobs sounds like a good trade-off when considering the jobs that were created.[47]

Targeted through Trello

Here at UCC, I've gradually sought out as many ways as possible to automate cumbersome, repetitive processes. One example where I've used automation is in my invoicing. We have hundreds of clients, each with many projects at various production stages. Manually producing an invoice for each completed product for each client can be a surprising time drain.

If you've already been involved with some aspect of business billing, you know that the process is not as simple as it might seem to someone unfamiliar with the progression. The person responsible for the billing needs to understand the timing components as well as the basic procedures. Here at UCC, every project is accompanied by a *job rider*. At each step along the production process, the person assigned to the task signs off when that step is completed.

Meanwhile, running parallel, the employee who makes the sale goes through the quoting and approval processes and writes the sales order, which generates the invoice. Early on, all the components of these processes were on paper and accompanied the project during each step in the processes. The system worked— like a horse and buggy worked to transport people throughout a late-nineteenth-century city. It was dependable, but it was also slow and sometimes sloppy. Today we use an efficient, automated cloud-based app called Trello.

With Trello, the completion of each step is tracked on automated index cards and checked off on a master card that follows the order through the whole process. There are no papers to lose, and there's no rush to compile all the info at the last minute. In a similar way, we've automated our work in progress (WIP) accounting and our inventory control procedures to accurately drive our production levels. At any given moment, I can view our current inventory and match it against our sales orders. This is all made possible by automation products that previous generations of business owners never had access to.

This does, however, come with a note of caution. As crucial as automation systems can be in improving efficiency, it's also important to consider and evaluate each process you intend to automate. Some processes aren't worth automating and can create inefficiency and waste.

Antiquated or Automated?

Without a doubt, automating any business is more cost effective and easier than ever to accomplish in the digital age. With easily accessible, uncomplicated software that can quickly automate a wide variety of time-consuming and mundane tasks, ignoring advancements can often be a huge mistake that places you at a great disadvantage against cutting-edge competitors.

If you've not done so already, automation is something you should consider immediately. Here are a few areas in which I've automated my company:

- *Invoicing*: When a job quote is created, the same spreadsheet produces all the different types of invoices we may need. For example, if a job has a deposit on it, we send a deposit invoice. The spreadsheet has a script that automatically produces a PDF and emails it to the salesperson. This automation has saved thousands of button clicks by producing all the information needed simultaneously.

- *Collection reminders*: When a job is moved to an invoiced status on our WIP sheet, it starts a timer. If the customer doesn't meet the terms, auto reminders are sent to the salesperson and accounting department so they know to make collection attempts. This is an escalating process that's fully automated.

- *Sales commissions*: When a salesperson makes a sale, they have a sheet to track their sales commissions. When the money is collected for the job, it triggers the sales commission to automatically be added to their next paycheck.

- *Shop floor information*: Also known as cut lists, assembly sheets are tailored for each individual area of the shop. We use the principles of LEAN for this process, which allows us to access the information we need as efficiently as possible. Most send out all the information for a specific job on one or two documents. The problem is there's information that may not be needed by someone later in the process. Instead, we created a set of seven documents that go with every job on the Trello card. Each area of the shop has only the information its operators need to complete their task and nothing else.

- *Delivery scheduling*: Once a job reaches a certain spot in the process, the delivery scheduling begins. The logistics of delivery can be extremely complex and hard to nail down. By the time the job is complete, we try to have a delivery day finalized so that the job sits in the warehouse for no more than two days. This is hard to do, but the trigger helps us make a delivery date with a high degree of certainty.

- *Work in process tracking without increasing administrative load on the shop*: We track where the jobs are in the process, but we don't require an employee *to job on/off*. Simply put, when a label is printed or a Trello card is moved, updates begin automatically. At any time, we can look at the WIP sheet and tell exactly where jobs are in the process.

- *Kanban for reordering materials*: There's nothing more frustrating than running out of product when you need it the most. Yet for some reason, it seems impossible to get employees to tell you when they're running out. This is why we create Kanban cards when we want something reordered. The card is hung on their workbench, much like a short-order cook hangs a ticket in the window when they holler, "Order up!" When the employee clocks out for the day, they take all the Kanban cards off the wire and drop them off at the office where the product is ordered. Once the order is made, the office returns the cards to the shop floor for the process to start all over.

- *Consolidated vendor invoicing to reduce data entry:* As UCC grew, I noticed that we received a tremendous number of invoices from our vendors. To solve this issue, I asked them all to consolidate them onto one invoice per week. Although some didn't because of limitations of their systems, most did, and it reduced data entry by about 35 percent.

- *Trello card movements based on prerequisites being complete:* We use an add-on called Butler to automate card movements within Trello. Once A and B are done, C happens. Again, this is all done without adding administrative load on the employees.

- *Google Drive file-storage templates:* Every time a new job number is created, we have a running script that creates a folder for that job. The folder has subfolders within it for things like CAD drawings, financials, drawings, and info notes. These folders have spreadsheets, PDFs, and other items we use for every job. But rather than create them for every job, we automated it.

Here are some other automations you might find helpful:

- *Email campaigns*: According to "35 Face-Melting Email Marketing Stats" on WordStream, "59% of B2B marketers say email is their most effective channel in terms of revenue generation."[48] So, don't sell email marketing short. *PC Magazine* listed "The Best Email Marketing Software for 2021," which included HubSpot, Constant Contact, Campaigner, and several more.[49] Best of all, some of them, such as HubSpot, offer free versions.

- *Direct mail campaigns*: According to Arthur Zuckerman in the article "40 Direct Mail Statistics: 2020/2021 Behavior, Trends & Data Analysis," "73% of American consumers say they prefer being contacted by brands via direct mail because they can read it whenever they want."[50] Postalytics is one company that can automate all your direct mail operations. After you've provided Postalytics the basics for your direct mail campaigns, all you need to do for each individual campaign is click a few buttons. They handle everything from there.

- *Payroll and time sheets*: QuickBooks lists "6 Key Benefits of Using Payroll Software for Small Businesses," including saving time and staying compliant with regulations.[51] Fit Small Business lists its "6 Best Free Payroll Software for 2021," which includes Time Trex, Payroll4Free.com, HR.my, Excel Payroll, Paycheck Manager, and eSmart Payroll.[52] And again, at least one of the services is free (as seen in its name)! Payroll is one of those activities that gets overlooked, but since every company has payroll, there are some great choices to fully automate it.

- *Human resources*: In "The 'Whys' of Why You Should Consider HR Software for Your Small Business," we find cost savings, better use of time, more accurate insights, and surprising cost effectiveness as reasons to invest in HR software.[53] Software Advice, Inc. offers a comprehensive listing of more than 1,000 human resources programs you can choose from to automate your HR needs.

- *Supply chain*: According to Kabbage by American Express, in the article "Supply Chain Management Software for Small Businesses,[54]" reduced shipment costs, error minimization, increased profitability, better customer service, and improved compliance rates are all good reasons to get supply chain software. Quick Sprout gives its recommendations for "Best Supply Chain Management Software," which includes the following:

  » *SAP SCM*: best for complex manufacturing,

  » *Anvyl*: best for small businesses with growth potential,

  » *Logility Solutions*: best for retail products and consumer goods,

  » *Hybrent*: best for healthcare professionals,

  » *ArrowStream*: best for the food service industry, and

  » *Fishbowl Inventory*: best for warehouse and manufacturing management.[55]

- *Expense management*: Expense OnDemand lists the following as good reasons to buy expense management software:

  » Eliminates human error

» Increases operational efficiency

» Improves spend visibility

» Enforces expense policies

» Speeds up approval and reimbursement

» Provides enhanced fraud prevention [56]

- Software Connect is a great site to check out as you shop for expense management software programs, as they offer a wide variety of choices.

Proficiency Pays Off for Patrons

Efficiency is not the end game. It's the means by which we provide our customers with both a high-quality product *and* an affordable price. For example, when a customer purchases a set of kitchen cabinets from UCC, they don't expect to pay for any inefficiencies in my company's processes. They just want the nicest, best-built set of cabinets they can get for the best possible price. But if even one step in my production process is inefficient, then that customer is paying for something more than just their cabinets—they're paying for my failure to run an efficient business.

For any business to achieve maximum efficiency, the employees must also buy into the LEAN-manufacturing philosophy. They're most likely to do so if their employer leads rather than pushes them into this philosophy. Do this by explaining how the idea works and why it benefits them just as much as it does the owner and the customers. Then lead by example. As I've put this philosophy into practice, I've seen some of my employees doing the same, looking for and implementing more efficient procedures. And as

I've mentioned before, teamwork must be a key element in your quest to fire yourself.

CHAPTER CHECKLIST

1. If you haven't already, begin making a list of your company's procedures that could be streamlined through automation.

2. Think through a process—beginning to end—for implementing automation in various processes.

3. Examine some business automation software programs, and see which ones might be of use to you.

4. How might you involve your employees—your team—in automating many of your company's processes?

ACTION ITEM: Choose one area where you could automate your systems with one of the latest business programs, such as the ones listed above. This will help you to compete on an equal footing with your competitors. Don't wait until tomorrow.

CHAPTER 7

DELEGATE OR DECLINE

Surround yourself with the best people you can find,
delegate authority, and don't interfere as long as the policy
you've decided upon is being carried out.
—Ronald Reagan[57]

DELEGATION CAN BE tough to get right, but it's essential for the fire-yourself process to run smoothly. It starts with the most trusted employees you already have and will eventually expand to more and more employees. Begin by asking each of your employees where they'd like to be within the company in three years. Where do they want to go? Are they happy with their current role and responsibilities?

Vanquish the Vicious Sales Cycle

In 2013, I decided we needed to make a big change in our business. I couldn't seem to get over that threshold of making the business bigger than myself and wore too many hats within the business. As soon as the business was close to that threshold, immediately we'd get knocked down a couple notches. What I soon realized was that we'd fallen prey to what I now call *the vicious sales cycle*.

The vicious sales cycle occurs when the owner runs both the sales and production side of the business. When the business slows, the owner is forced to sell more products or services. During this period, production slumps and profits increase from the work completed during the last cycle. Once the business lands all the work from sales, the opposite begins to happen. Production rises, cash flow decreases, and sales decline because you're in the shop or the office producing.

Recognizing the pattern was my aha moment, and I began to research what other companies were doing to solve the problem. I landed on the idea of hiring an executive business coach. After interviewing several coaches, I chose Martin Holland from right here in Oklahoma. Martin understood manufacturing, so we didn't have to spend time helping him learn the processes and got right to work streamlining the business. Several years later, Martin and I continue to push past thresholds and overcome new challenges.

One of the first things Martin helped me see was that I needed to delegate duties and be able to work *on* the business, not just *in* it. If I could get the daily shop floor grind off my list of responsibilities, then the business could soar. I'd assumed previously that I was the driving force behind the business because I could produce products so efficiently. In reality, being the top producer consumed most of my focus, and I neglected the business of my business. I realized that this had to change, and fast.

Like many owners, I wore too many hats. I worked on the shop floor, sold, balanced the books, and more. I spun my wheels at 100 mph but got almost nowhere. I was the problem because I was trying to do everything. Sometimes in business you just need to get out of your own way to hurdle the next barrier in front of you. For a business to thrive, it must be able to function properly without much input from you.

The Shift: Start Small

When it comes to delegating, remember to start small. I didn't, and that mistake set me back. Once I finally decided to delegate responsibilities, I started with the one thing that held me back the most, which was the production work on the shop floor. With the daily production off my plate, I was able to quit working on the shop floor. At first, things went ok. But after a few days, the questions began to roll in, and I realized this was not going to be an easy transition.

We had no systems or SOPs to answer all the questions and no structure in place because it was all just day-to-day operating. The way I chose to do things was how we functioned. That method had to change, and I knew I needed to delegate. But rather than delegating an entire function or system, I needed to delegate individual tasks that made up the system. A key element in achieving this level of delegation is to have easily understood and accessible SOPs like the ones discussed in chapter three.

I began delegating by giving an employee three relatively simple, manageable tasks. This method became my SOP for delegating. Once the employee had those three tasks completed or mastered, I gave him or her three more tasks. Eventually this process had a snowball effect, as employees then delegated to others. Whether it's on the shop floor or in managerial tasks, gradually but increasingly trust your employees with more duties to take the workload off yourself.

Though it might seem obvious, some duties are not transferable between job positions. Most shop floor production workers wouldn't do well taking on the role of accountant—or vice versa. But a responsible, long-term production worker probably will do an excellent job of training a new production worker in the position's specific duties and overall production process. Why should you, the owner, spend hours teaching a new hire when those hours could be devoted to expanding your business— especially when your best shop floor employees could fill that role admirably?

Trust but Verify—and Train Tirelessly

So, you've hired top-notch managers and employees, written your SOPs, established a good work environment, and are beginning the delegation process. The next step is to trust but verify.

No matter how responsible and trustworthy your managers and employees are, they're still humans, and humans make mistakes. At times, they may even give in to the temptation of taking shortcuts. In my estimation, periodically verifying the proper completion of tasks is a valuable use of an owner's time. I like to relate this verification concept to a dentist coming in at the end of a cleaning. After the hygienist completes the X-rays, cleaning, and polishing, the dentist comes in for a final check. I've learned over the years that failing to complete this verification step can be costly.

One way we achieve this verification step is through weekly all-hands meetings in which everyone on the shop floor discusses what's going well and what might be improved. It's mostly just a time to fix little issues before they become big problems and a chance to keep the team focused on the company vision.

A process we've found beneficial in these all-hands meetings is a game in which we line up all the staff members in our places within the production process. For us, the CNC machine is first, then the edge bander, and so on. Then we play what we call *the customer game*, because we've learned that it's hard for someone at the beginning or middle of the production process to have a direct relationship with our paying customers.

To accomplish this, we break the process down into smaller components and have our employees look at the next person in line as their customer. Making that connection helps each worker see how they can improve the customer's purchasing experience. We can play this game down the line all the way to the delivery. Once we're there, we start over, and each person asks their next-in-line customer, "Is there anything I can do to make your job easier or improve your product?" From this procedure, we've learned little things, like orienting a part a certain way before the piece goes to the next station. Something this small and simple can improve efficiency and build a team environment.

Releasing Responsibilities: Reluctantly or Resolutely?

Delegating duties within your business can be akin to giving your children more responsibilities and freedoms as they mature. The first time you allow your five-year-old to walk two blocks to kindergarten, your heart is pounding, and you find it hard to think of anything else until he or she returns home a few hours later. The next day, the anxiety is a bit less intense, and each successive day brings you greater confidence in their increasing responsibility.

Once responsibility is further proven over the years, when it's time to take a driver's license test, you trust your child to be conscientious in this new phase. The same can be said when it's time to choose a career or a life partner, and you'll have to trust in your child's ability to use good judgment. Trusting your employees to diligently discharge more of the responsibilities you'd previously handled is a step-by-step process not unlike raising a family. If you're training them properly, you can delegate confidently as you progress toward the goal of firing yourself.

Trusting and Testing

As an owner with the goal of firing myself, learning to trust my employees by testing their abilities and their willingness to take on new or expanded roles is an ongoing challenge—one I'm learning as I go. I once had an employee named Tyler who was instrumental in helping me achieve this balance between giving good employees new tasks and overburdening them. Unfortunately, learning that lesson came at the cost of losing him, both as a valued employee and friend.

I hired Tyler in 2009 as my business rebounded following the great recession. Tyler didn't always follow my mantra of "worker smarter, not harder," but he did indeed always work hard and was always willing to take on new tasks. So, when two of my best employees moved away, rather than hiring two replacements, I gave Tyler the opportunity to take on their roles. Given his admirable work ethic, Tyler dutifully pursued the added responsibilities, and I went on about my business of running the business.

But soon I began to see the business run into numerous snags, and all those snags pointed back to Tyler. He wasn't keeping up, and rather than realizing that I'd piled too many responsibilities onto Tyler's plate, I began to snipe at this well-meaning worker. Eventually Tyler broke. He'd had enough of my criticisms and resigned. It was only then that I saw how unfairly I'd treated Tyler. He moved away, and it was too late for me to undo my mistake, but it was not too late for me to learn from that mistake.

Yes, a key component in achieving the goal of firing oneself is to increasingly delegate duties to trusted employees. But owners also need to remember that it's possible to delegate too much too fast. The process of delegating needs to be gradual and strategic, not hasty and impulsive.

Amy was another excellent worker who caught my eye because of her dedication to her specific duties and her eagerness to take on new roles. Since she successfully took on each new assignment I gave her, I soon felt confident in placing her in a management role, where she has thrived and been a great asset in the company.

On the other hand, Brianna came to work for us at about the same time as Amy and didn't work out in the same way. Although she also quickly exhibited a great work ethic and aptitude, Brianna had no such aspirations to step into a managerial role. She excelled at her job on the production line and was more than happy to stay there.

Working with diverse people has taught me the need to be a flexible owner and boss. I've come to appreciate the uniqueness of individuals and to be sensitive to their personality types—a topic we'll examine a bit later. The key for me is learning more about how to incorporate each unique trait a person might have and maximize it in order to build a cohesive team.

CHAPTER CHECKLIST

1. Ask each of your employees where they'd like to be within the company in three years, where they want to go, and if they're happy with their current role and responsibilities.

2. Examine your role in your company. Do you see "the vicious sales cycle" as the go-to process? Are you ready to change that process?

3. Can you identify one or more of your employees who are reliable enough to begin taking on new tasks?

4. As you delegate, what are some ways you can verify that tasks are being properly completed?

5. What's the first task you'd like to delegate? Who within your company might have the right skill set to take on that task?

ACTION ITEM: Pick a reliable employee and delegate an appropriate task to him or her, making sure to fully explain the task and your expectations. Then evaluate the employee's performance. Once you've done so, congratulate yourself. You've taken a big step toward firing yourself.

CHAPTER 8

YOUR STRONG RIGHT HAND

It is absolutely necessary therefore for me to have persons
that can think for me, as well as execute orders.
—George Washington[58]

GENERAL GEORGE WASHINGTON wanted "persons that could think for [him]." Unfortunately, Washington's second-in-command during the Revolutionary War wanted to think a bit too much—and mostly for himself. General Charles Lee fancied himself a better soldier and strategist than Washington, his designated superior. Lee—who favored guerrilla-style militia tactics over Washington's choice of a more formal, centralized army—repeatedly sought to undermine and replace his boss. At the Battle of Monmouth, Lee led his troops in a retreat rather than advancing as Washington had ordered, running straight into Washington and his advancing army. Following the battle, Lee was "court-martialed and found guilty of disobedience, misbehavior before the enemy, shameful retreat, and disrespect to the commander-in-chief."[59]

Designating Your Deputy

Charles Lee is an obvious example of a second-in-command most business owners will want to avoid. Instead, we want to choose those who exhibit the loyalty, selflessness, and competence of Moses's Aaron, Batman's Robin, or Frodo's Samwise. Here are five of the top qualities I look for in a second-in-command:

1. *Loyalty*. No doubt this quality is obvious and intuitive. Loyalty is exactly the character quality Washington's direct subordinate lacked. A loyal person is quick to obey and defend, while being slow to suspect, oppose, or criticize the person to whom his or her loyalty is directed. A loyal person is usually willing to make sacrifices for the person to whom his or her loyalty is directed. A loyal chief deputy can be counted on to respect his or her leader, carry out the leader's commands, and give good advice. The chief deputy must be loyal not only to the owner but also to the company's vision statement.

2. *Honesty*. This quality counterbalances the first. Unconstrained loyalty borders on cultism and is of little to no use to an honest and self-confident boss. A good chief deputy can be counted on to be courageous enough to challenge the boss if he or she thinks the boss is about to make a decision detrimental to the company's best interests. But the chief deputy also needs the next trait.

YOUR STRONG RIGHT HAND

3. *Humility*: He or she needs to keep in mind that the owner—who has the most to gain or to lose—has the final say in any business decision. A good chief deputy understands that unless specifically assigned a decision-making role in a given situation, he or she is an adviser and facilitator and not the final authority.

4. *Discretion*: A chief deputy is likely to be privy to business discussions and negotiations that other staff members need not know about until decisions are finalized. A gossipy person will not do well as a second-in-command.

5. *Knowledge*: Not to be overlooked, of course, is high-level knowledge of the business. Goals, production processes and practices, environment and culture, employee and hiring practices, and disciplinary practices are all things that need to be effectively understood to run the business in the owner's absence.

In essence, the chief deputy is a go-between as well as a trusted colleague and confidant. His or her first loyalty must be to the owner, but he or she must also be an advocate for the employees. Consequently, your second-in-command will be key in developing your team culture.

Additionally, according to Cameron Herold, the former chief operating officer of 1-800-GOT-JUNK?, a business owner who's considering hiring a second-in-command needs to "be honest with yourself about what your weaknesses are and identify the areas of the job you don't love doing so you can find someone who has strengths in those areas and enjoys those aspects of the business."[60] In other words, a good chief deputy needs to know not only how to fill in for you in your absence but also excel in the areas in which you prefer to avoid. For example, if you're happy to pay your employees but have no patience for administering the payroll process, finding a second-in-command who enjoys that type of administrative duty might be an important consideration.

Pursuing the Proper Personality Type

Psychologists have designated four distinct personality types of which every person can be categorized. Type A people tend to be goal-oriented risk-takers who handle pressure well. If you're a *Star Trek* fan, think Captain Kirk or Captain Picard. Not surprisingly, folks who start their own businesses tend to be Type A. Type B people tend to be relationship oriented and extroverted. Think Doctor McCoy or Neelix. Type C people tend to be logical, detail oriented, and dependable. Think Mr. Spock or Seven of Nine. Type D tend to be task oriented and stable but also cautious. Think of Chief Engineer Scott. Which of those personality types would seem to be best suited to filling the role of a second-in-command? Which of those personality types would seem to mesh best with your personality type and work preferences at your business?

At first glance, a Type C might seem like an ideal fit for a chief-deputy role. What business owner would not want a second-in-command who is logical, detail oriented, and dependable? But on the flip side, a Type C can be skeptical and critical of others who don't share his or her high standards. Those with this personality type can appear aloof, detached, and stubborn. So, if you're considering a Type C for your chief deputy, you'll need to weigh that person's logic, meticulousness, and dependability against his or her possible hinderance to team building.

On the other hand, a Type B could be a great asset in building a cohesive team, but he or she might lack some of the precision and reliability you'll need from someone who will be assuming your command-level responsibilities in your absence. Unfortunately, there's no simple answer for finding the perfect second-in-command. Perhaps, as you search for the ideal person, the sunshine will break through the clouds and a halo glow of divine approval will reveal itself on your ideal sidekick as a Morgan Freeman–like voice declares, "This is the Chosen One." But it's far more likely that you'll have to spend a lot of time searching for the right person. But don't give up or get discouraged. Finding that person is a key component in your effort to fire yourself.

When you finally do find your ideal chief deputy, your next question likely will be, "If I do find someone of such high-caliber qualities, can I afford to pay him or her enough to join me?" For a struggling start-up, coming up with enough regular income to appropriately compensate a highly qualified number two might seem unattainable. And that might indeed be true, at least for the first few months or years. But at some point, after pouring long hours and days into building your dream business, any owner will need someone to provide the kind of support only a trusted and qualified second-in-command can provide. Having a dedicated, competent chief deputy is important enough to consider some creative compensation.

Creative Compensations

Obviously, your chief deputy will need to be someone who believes in your business. A person might have all the qualities you're looking for, but if he or she lacks faith in you and your business model, the relationship will not go far. Assuming your choice for chief does indeed share your passion for and confidence in the business, you might be able to persuade him or her to accept a modest salary and benefits package coupled with a share of the profits.

Here are a few suggestions from online resources you can use to establish a profit-sharing plan for your business that incentivizes business growth:

"Profit-Sharing Plans for Small Businesses"[61]

"How to Create a Profit-Sharing Plan"[62]

"The 3 Approaches to Profit-Sharing"[63]

Along those lines but with a twist, consider writing out a contract outlining incentive-based raises. Similar to the profit-sharing plan, with this method the chief deputy (or others) sees his or her salary rise commensurate with annual profits. If the company's profits grow by 10 percent for the year, the chief deputy gets a designated percent raise for the coming year.

My Second-in-Command

Briton came to me fresh off completing his associate degree when he was still a teenager trying to figure out what to do with his life. Because of his youth and inexperience, I started him as my "catch guy," and his job was to simply catch the pieces I cut and stack them on the cart to be hauled to the next station in the production process. Yes, it was a menial task, but he was young and inexperienced.

But it didn't take long for Briton to show competence and initiative. When he saw ways to help me or improve efficiency, he didn't hesitate to implement those improvements. And those deeds didn't escape my notice. I continued to give him bigger responsibilities, which he always accomplished. Of course, I rewarded him for those improvements, and that, in turn, motivated him to continue his excellent work. Over time, Briton gradually grew into the role of my second-in-command.

What I especially appreciated about Briton was that he never asked for a raise. Instead, he regularly approached me with questions about what he could do to take tasks off my plate to help me get to the next level. If that meant he needed to delegate some of his tasks to free room on his plate, he was willing to do that.

But the day arrived when Briton felt he needed to move his family to another town 90 miles away, which was too far for a daily commute. In turn, Briton sorrowfully resigned. Valuing his commitment to the company and his work ethic, I quickly decided I needed to be creative and find a way to keep him with the company despite his move. I decided to lease a building in the town he moved to and provided all the equipment Briton would need in order to build cabinets right there in his new location. He did so well there that soon he had five employees working for him at the new shop.

After a few years, Briton decided it was time to move his family back to Collinsville and resume his role as my right-hand man—a role he earned and has handled admirably. After going through this experience, my advice is to pay attention. Your second-in-command might already be in your shop or office.

CHAPTER CHECKLIST

1. What tangible traits would you look for in trying to determine a potential chief deputy's loyalty?

2. How is your track record when assessing another person's honesty?

3. Are you quick to accurately assess another person's humility? Can you think of some examples when you did so?

4. Discretion is an important characteristic for your second-in-command. What might be some ways to test a potential colleague's discretion?

5. What would be the best way to test a potential chief deputy's knowledge of your type of business?

6. Which elements of your business are, rather than a fun challenge, a chore you'd rather assign to a right-hand man or woman?

7. Have you considered which personality type would best mesh with your personality and business philosophy?

8. Look for creative ways to recruit and keep a loyal chief deputy. Choose one who will help you achieve your goal of firing yourself.

ACTION ITEM: If you don't yet have a designated second-in-command, start evaluating who you will select. Set a date to make that selection. If you do have that person, take a moment to express your gratitude for his or her loyalty and reliability.

CHAPTER 9

CRAMMING FOR INESCAPABLE CRISES

If something can go wrong, it will.
—Murphy's Law

THERE'S NO POINT in being pessimistic; it wouldn't work anyway. Yes, the t-shirt with that annoyingly appropriate adage about pessimism became so trendy that when you went to buy one on Amazon, you discovered it was all sold out. You knew that would happen.

This is how it goes. You get pumped for a great day that will be highlighted by a midmorning meeting with a potential new client. Then it starts. First, you drop your breakfast toast, and it predictably lands on your new white carpet, grape-jelly side down.

Then you forget to shave and remember you can't show up to that meeting with the potential client appearing too casual with two days' worth of stubble. Naturally, you also forgot to charge your rechargeable shaver overnight. After several minutes of searching, you find a little disposable razor and manage to get a decent shave with just one noticeable nick. You're still okay because you've only lost 10 minutes and can make that up on the drive to the office with a little luck.

With just half a mile to go, you've made up more than eight of those 10 minutes. Then, directly in front of you, a delivery truck jackknifes on a patch of ice and spills its entire load of hot dogs, right alongside Ken's Keeshond Kennels housing dozens of yipping, yowling, and hungry hounds whose highly sensitive noses have scented the succulent sausages. While all that might seem humorous, it isn't funny for the hard-working delivery drivers who've lost their wieners. Or for you when you realize you might lose that once-in-a-lifetime client who has no interest in your lame story about your drive being delayed by a ton of wayward weenies and two desperate delivery drivers trying to round up all those fallen franks.

Murphy Hates Honchos

As tough as Murphy is in general, I've found that his exasperating law seems to have special jurisdiction within the workings of small, independent businesses like mine. If you've run your business for more than a week, I'm sure you know what I mean. And because of the many things that can go wrong that are all too often unforeseeable, you, as the head honcho, have to be the ultimate on-the-spot problem solver.

Realistically, you can't anticipate and prepare for any and every challenge that might arise. But what you can and must do is learn from each of them. As I hinted at before, the key to defeating Murphy is to turn trivial troubles into team triumphs before they become huge hindrances.

After we've weathered that storm, it would be easy to reason that everything is ok, and then push forward with business as usual. But giving into that temptation will almost certainly mean we'll face that same production-hindering hurdle again—and perhaps repeatedly. Addressing the issue head-on the first time and then creating an SOP to refer to later will save loads of time, and time is money.

Crisis or Complication?

Before examining ways to deal with crises, we should consider the difference between a genuine crisis and an everyday complication. A mere complication is something that's not detrimental to the long-term function of the business. For example, if a cabinet fails to fit together properly because a part is not cut correctly, that's a complication. The business isn't going to fail because one part is cut incorrectly. However, that problem left unattended could ultimately affect the proper running of the company in an expanded way.

An owner who's not relentless about fixing mundane issues will see those issues grow into crises. For example, in 2014 we'd finally recovered from the recession that began in 2008 and were beginning to grow again. We had about 12 employees and more work than we knew what to do with. I was wearing many hats, as usual, but my primary focus was sales, so production quality began to decline. I was oblivious to the decline because my employees were not telling me about little issues as they happened. Instead, they were letting problems slide or attempting to fix issues as they saw fit without the bigger picture in mind.

One day I got a call from a fuming customer who had never before complained. He was so upset that he was ready to find another company to buy from. I dropped everything and went to meet him on his job site. What I saw was gut wrenching. It was a pile of little issues, imperfections here and there. Individually, the problems were not too serious. However, taken as a whole, it appeared as if we had no idea what we were doing. After working out a deal to address the situation, I left the job confident I'd put out the fire. But no sooner than I'd started up my truck did another customer call with almost identical issues. Four similar phone calls followed shortly after.

These were seemingly small problems that had been compounded to the point of putting my company in serious jeopardy. To fix the immediate issues, I closed the shop for three days and sent each employee to the job sites one at a time until everything was fixed and the customers were happy. Fortunately, because of our quick response, I didn't lose any customers. Moving forward, we put a system in place that required either me or the manager directly involved to be notified of any small issue before it could erupt into a crisis. The issue is either fixed if needed or approved by a manager. The employee is then not put in the position of having to make a judgement call on something that might end up as a customer complaint.

Three *D*s of Directing Beyond Disaster

No business owner can predict precisely what each and every coming crisis will look like. But we can prepare for them in general terms by establishing a crisis plan that outlines key principles for dealing with any potential calamity. That principle-based plan can be created by learning from the mistakes of others.

Here are my three *D*s for dealing with any crisis (present or future):

1. *Demonstrate humility.* By this, I mean admit your mistakes, personal and corporate. When we make costly mistakes, our natural inclination is to try to hide or cover them up. Anyone over age 60 is likely familiar enough with the Watergate scandal to remember that it was President Nixon's attempts to cover up the Watergate break-in and not the break-in itself that cost him his presidency. Similarly, if in 1998 President Clinton had come forward and admitted the truth when the Monica Lewinsky scandal broke, he likely wouldn't have faced an impeachment trial. If your company makes a bad decision that hurts your customers or the community, admit it and then explain through the media what you'll do to set things right. Do exactly what you said you'd do, no matter how much it hurts.

2. *Double down on your commitment to your vision statement.* More than likely, when you or your company make mistakes, it'll be because you lost track of your vision statement. Problems pop up when focus is misdirected. Focusing on profits first is a sure way to invite troubles into your business. If you take care of your people, they will take care of the business. Guide your employees to the

direction of the vision statement, and that focus will bring the profits.

3. *Develop a crisis management plan.* This step is more difficult than the first two and requires a lot of forward thinking, so it might be wise to recruit one or more of your staff members to help you brainstorm. The idea is to think through as many crisis scenarios as possible. When you've identified the possibilities, walk through the best ways to handle them based primarily on the principles seen in steps one and two above.

Elements of a Crisis Management Plan

I wish I could lay out, step-by-step, everything you'll need to do to develop the crisis management plan (CMP) perfectly suited to your business. But a one-size-fits-all CMP is not possible. Each business is unique, and the potential crises each business will face are as varied as the myriad of products and services offered by the millions of America's small businesses. If you can afford to do so, I'd suggest you hire a consultant to guide your team through the process of developing a CMP. If hiring a consultant is too expensive, here are some articles that can provide some guidance when creating your CMP:

- Centre Technology's "Elements of an Effective Crisis Management Plan"[64]

- "PR Newswire's CMP Elements"[65]

Remember as you work through these steps that your ultimate goal is to fire yourself. To get there, you'll need employee buy-in to be prepared to successfully deal with any crisis. And the best way to get that employee buy-in is to develop the team concept we explored in chapter four.

Experiencing Emotional Equilibrium

It's also worth noting that navigating through crises is about more than merely coming out financially solvent on the other side. It's also about maintaining your and your team's emotional balance. To that end, humor can be a beneficial balm. Following your postcrisis analysis, consider calling the team together to unwind while watching a mindless, funny movie, like two of my favorites, *Dumb and Dumber* or *Wayne's World*. Or maybe just tell a few jokes. Here are a few business-related jokes from *Reader's Digest*:

- To resolve conflicts between management and staff, I brought both sides together and asked employees to jot down key words on a flip chart. One participant complained about management's tendency to interfere and wrote the word *nitpicking*. A manager leaped to his feet to ask, "Shouldn't there be a hyphen between nit and picking?" – E. Howson, in *Reader's Digest International Edition*

- Our booking office had three phones. One day during lunch, I was responsible for answering all of them. It was a constant repeat of "May I help you?" or "Will you hold?" I guess I got confused because I surprised one man on the other end of the line when I answered his call with "May I hold you?" – Vera Granger

- The printer was broken, and no one could figure out whose fault it was. After arguing back and forth, our supervisor took charge. "Look," he said, "we really don't need to determine who is responsible for this mess. We just want someone to take the blame."[66]

When things can seem like the end of the world, I like to keep this quote by H. G. Wells in mind: "The crisis of today is the joke of tomorrow."[67]

CHAPTER CHECKLIST

1. As stated in this chapter, addressing an issue head-on the first time, and then creating an SOP to refer to later, will save us loads of time, and time is money. Can you recall a situation in your business when you failed to address a potentially problematic issue head-on the first time and paid a heavy price for doing so?

2. Can you think of a time when you or someone close to you made a bad situation worse by trying to cover it up? Imagine now that same situation, but picture yourself or that friend admitting the mistake right up front.

3. If you've not yet written your vision statement, this would be a good time to begin. As you do, consider how it might help you prevent small snags from becoming business-threatening crises.

4. Creating a CMP can have great value. Now is the perfect time to consider who you might invite to help in brainstorming that plan.

5. Have you experienced humor as "a beneficial balm"—even in dark times?

ACTION ITEM: If you haven't developed a CMP, get started. Set a completion date and get to work.

|————————————————————————————————|

CHAPTER 10

PUSH THRU: PERSISTENCE PAYS

Pressure drives progress.
—Jeff Finney

YOU ESTABLISHED A spot-on vision statement so that you know precisely where you want to take your business. You've hired excellent employees, including a sharp, dedicated second-in-command. You've created a team-first culture with top-notch employees. You've written your SOPs, giving your team members the autonomy they need to function efficiently within the team concept. All that preparation and dedication and still those crises, as mentioned in the previous chapter, have pummeled your business, placing you on the precipice of capitulation. Sometimes, the only thing you can do is persist, despite repeated setbacks.

Harriet Tubman, Persistent Overcomer

Araminta Ross was born between 1820 and 1822 on a slave plantation in Maryland. She preferred the name Harriet, the name that she gave herself when she married John Tubman, a free Black man, in 1844.[68] When Harriet was still quite young, her slave owner sold her three older sisters to another slave owner. She never saw those sisters again. But she persisted. Young Harriet, then the oldest of the remaining Ross children, had to take on the role of caregiver to her younger siblings as her parents worked long hours in the fields.[69]

Before she reached adulthood, Harriet's back was covered with scars from repeated whippings. Once when a slave owner threw an iron weight at another enslaved person, it missed and hit Harriet in the head. As a result, she suffered seizures throughout the rest of her life. But she persisted.[70] In 1849, Harriet made the second of her escapes from slavery and its atrocities. Though she succeeded, it was not long afterward that John Tubman married another woman.[71] But she persisted. And despite these many hardships, Harriet Tubman became the American Moses, helping untold numbers of enslaved people escape bondage via the famous Underground Railroad.[72]

No one in the modern American business world has ever or will ever face the extreme trials Harriet Tubman overcame. But as we face our own lesser trials, we can take inspiration from Harriet Tubman's example of persistence.

Edison's Successful Failures

According to Leonard DeGraaf's book *Edison and the Rise of Innovation*, Thomas "Edison's not a guy that looks back. Even for his biggest failures he didn't spend a lot of time wringing his hands and saying, 'Oh my God, we spent a fortune on that.' He said, 'We had fun spending it.' "[73]

As business owners, sometimes we, like Thomas Edison, have to take our failures in stride, seeing each of those failures as a building block rather than as a stumbling stone. This famous quote of his about failure couldn't be more fitting or inspirational. "Results! Why, man, I have gotten a lot of results! I know several thousand things that won't work."[74]

My Lucky Launch

I started my business in 2005 with a 50-50 business partner. During the first few years, we grew rapidly. Within a few months, we were at a $500,000 per year run rate. Basically, we went from $0 to $50k per month in the matter of a few months. As you might imagine, we were flyin' high.

But this early success was superficial. We were not growing a company—it was just a really big hobby. The difference between a hobby and a business is a stark one. A business should make money; hobbies just cost money. Every dollar that came into the company went right back out in the form of either salary or debt payments. We were not building the foundation for our company properly, and that would come back to bite us when the recession took hold. More about that a little later.

I tried to run the company as a side hustle for as long as I could, but it wasn't long before I felt I was cheating my full-time job. Just four years before, I'd graduated from college and went to work for a reputable company in Tulsa. I had a great job working as a project superintendent on large-scale construction projects, and I really liked it. I stayed with that job for the next five years, and it wasn't until a unique opportunity crossed my path that I considered leaving.

It began when I started to tinker with furniture. One of my old college buddies saw my work and asked me to build his kitchen cabinets, and I reluctantly said yes. I had a small garage and built two or three cabinets at a time, storing them in the guest room of my house while I built a couple more. After that project, I continued to build cabinets for that same friend's builder in Stillwater, a nearby town.

Shortly after, I made the best dumb choice I'd ever rendered. My business partner at the time was given an opportunity to bid on a 62-unit multifamily project that was so far out of our league we had no business even considering it. Each unit had four bedrooms and four bathrooms, plus a large utility room and kitchen per side. Somehow, we managed to get through the project, and it provided us with a valuable learning experience. Just imagine the terror of being awarded a $600,000 project in your first year when your company consists of just three people—two of whom had full-time employment elsewhere. There's no other feeling quite like such a simultaneous mix of excitement and terror.

The Conundrum: Secure Supporter or Vulnerable Vendor?

Shortly after we were awarded the duplex project, I knew I had to make a very difficult decision about my full-time job. Leaving that job would be difficult for obvious reasons, like money and security. But ultimately, I left a good-paying job for a business start-up with no guarantee of any income. Yet somehow, even in the toughest times, I've never regretted going out and making my own course. People who've been through similar circumstances might also look back at and wish they'd made that decision even earlier. I'll never regret taking the big leap.

During our first few years, we took the normal path to growth. Our primary focus was to grow at all costs. We just needed to sell, sell, sell, and worry later about how to fulfill all those sales. Our entire mindset was geared around growth because at our profit levels we couldn't sustain any kind of owner salary. So out of what we thought was necessity, we grew at all costs.

We learned the basics of how to do payroll on our own, just to understand the system. We also did research on a regular basis to learn things like what tools larger companies used because we knew we were going to be growing for years to come.

One of my first tasks was to create a reliable cut-listing program so that we could cut parts quickly without having to figure out what part sizes were in our heads. A cut-list program takes what you want to build and gives you the dimensions of all the pieces that need to be cut. To do this, I made a very crude spreadsheet that you could plug the cabinet specifics into, and it would spit out several worksheet pages that had cut lists for every area. The four of us would take these cut lists to our respective areas and cut out all the parts for the cabinets and the doors.

One can only imagine how this home-brewed system worked, especially at this early stage. Several times I thought about just throwing it out altogether, but instead I persisted and made it better. This was due in large part to the alternative, which was a full-blown cabinet-design software program that cost $10,000. Because we weren't willing to settle for some of the cheaper alternatives, we stuck to our guns and made the spreadsheet work for the first few years. You can bet that as soon as we had enough money to buy that cabinet-design software, we jumped at the opportunity.

I often refer to these early years of our business as "brute-force awkwardness," because that's basically what it was. We were growing by any means necessary, and to us, that meant more frequently working with metaphorical hammers than with metaphorical scalpels. Whether it was trying to sell more product than we had the capacity to manufacture or working on our systems to make them more efficient, we did whatever we could to push forward.

This stage is one I believe all business owners should have to go through. Every owner should have to fully realize the pressure it takes to toe the line every day and face a pass-or-fail proposition. In fact, it's likely that most business owners don't have or even want venture capital to start our business. I, for one, am a firm believer that too much seed money raises the risk of failure, as too much money provides a false sense of security—a soft blanket to fall on when times get tough.

Rebounding from the Recession

It seems that with a lot of great success stories, somewhere along the way there was a pivotal moment or a significant low point that served as ground zero for rebuilding. In our case, that came late in the recession in 2010 and 2011.

In the beginning, even though the economy had begun to spiral downward, we had a ton of work and were the most profitable we'd ever been. To be honest, we never thought the recession fallout was going to be as bad as it was. Part of this is because there'd never been a significant downturn in my lifetime prior to this, and the great recession didn't seem like a realistic possibility. So, when the media spoke of a downturn in the economy, I just thought of it as a ripple in the water. I didn't know it was going to bring on a tsunami of economic change.

The downturn didn't hit my company until 2010. I watched as other businesses went belly up, but as my business chugged along, I conjured up this 18-foot-tall, bulletproof mentality that we'd succeed where others were failing. Reality didn't strike until the day one of our biggest customers told me their business had slowed significantly and that if we wanted to retain their business, we'd have to decrease our prices so they could remain competitive. The problem with that proposal was that we had no room left to go down in price. In fact, we were getting ready to tell them we needed to increase prices. As a result, we chose to finish the work we had on the books and part ways with one of our biggest accounts.

This turned out to be a defining moment for our company. We were forced to ditch our biggest contract and most consistent work because it was no longer profitable. It was the toughest decision we'd had to make and was also the precise moment that we started our own rapid decline to the bottom. Before long, it was all we could do to scrape up payroll, make our debt service payments, and keep the lights on. It was the worst time in my life that I can remember.

A Difficult Decision

First, we decided that there was no longer enough meat on the bone to support two owners. One of us would have to step aside. My business partner ultimately decided to leave and pursue another field, which turned out to be a great decision for him. I stayed put and attempted to weather the storm and make something out of the company I was so passionate about. However, it didn't take long to realize that even with dramatically reduced costs I needed more financial help. It pains me to admit, but during my darkest hour, I was out of choices and needed to lean on my family for financial help. Looking back, I can see that my business wouldn't have survived had my father not agreed to provide much-needed support.

As hard as it is for me to admit, I feel it's relevant because it's a huge part of my story. It's the basis that our company was rebuilt on. Because even without the recession, the company would not be open today had we not figured out how to really run a business. Until that point, we had no real structure and were simply running the business day by day, job by job.

The lowest point for the business came at the end of 2010. We had no jobs booked, zero prospects, and basically no cash reserves. With a mountain of bills looming, it seemed likely that we would not survive into the next year. We normally shut down from Christmas to New Year's, and that year, it was much needed, as we had no work. When the crew left for break, I told them to call me before returning so I could let them know if they'd still have their jobs.

Fortunately, the day after Christmas we got a call from a customer that wanted a kitchen remodel. As it turned out, it was just what we needed to survive and was our company's initial rebuilding block. Even writing this now, it's hard for me to go back and think about what would've happened if I hadn't received that call. I just don't know if we would've survived many more days or weeks without it. But from there we started to relearn how to run a business. We figured out how to get over the fear of the recession and not allow it to be a limiting factor in our own growth. And if I learned nothing else, I realized the role a limiting mindset can have on a business, and ultimately, it was our decision to choose to push through.

CHAPTER CHECKLIST

1. In the chapter, I discussed how starting out our mindset was growth at all costs because our profit levels couldn't sustain owner salary. Has this been your pattern for your start-up? If so, what problems can you see that philosophy causing you?

2. You might disagree with the statement "too much money provides a false sense of security, a soft blanket to fall on when times get tough." If you do disagree, write out the reasons for your disagreement.

3. What are some daunting challenges you've faced throughout your life? How did you push through those challenges, and how might analyzing your reactions to those past challenges help you conquer future challenges?

ACTION ITEM: Write out this note and place it on your desk or workstation: *Challenges are tests, not defeats.*

CHAPTER 11

THREE KEYS TO CUSTOMER SATISFACTION

Quality is not an act. It is a habit.
—Will Durant, paraphrasing Aristotle[75]

LESSONS CAN COME in many forms. I've learned that if I stay humble and ask questions, then I can learn more than I might have otherwise. I am also of the belief that you don't truly learn a lesson until the lesson is put into practice.

Once we had a local customer who'd ordered cabinet boxes and decided to have us assemble them in our shop so that he could install them himself. After delivery, the customer needed a little assistance getting started, so I offered to help. After going on-site,

I had a great conversation with the homeowner and learned he was a retired quality process engineer. I'd hit the jackpot!

This eventually led to him visiting the shop for a walk-through. The man kicked me into overdrive, forcing me to think about quality and building great processes in ways I'd not given much thought to.

Here are some of the key takeaways I gained from this surprise encounter with a quality process engineer that can help transform your shop:

- Get customer feedback.

- Make "kits" sooner.

- $1, $10, $100 (errors cost more later).

Get Customer Feedback

Taking the time to solicit and analyze customer feedback can seem like a waste of time to a business owner who already has five more jobs coming right at him. However, before we can set or adjust our quality standards, we need to establish a benchmark for those standards. We need to ask the very people we're creating value for about the product they received.

If this thought scares you, even a little, then I'd recommend immediately calling your last five customers for feedback. Whether it's good or bad, this is information you need to have.

Net Promoter Score (NPS) can help you set up a quick, easy survey if you don't already have something ready. Remember, it doesn't need to be anything fancy for the customer to give you the necessary feedback.

When choosing your five, don't just cherry-pick the good ones. Get a good mix so you can make an accurate assessment of where you're starting from. If you don't know the truth, you can't form a plan to improve. Or, as Yogi Berra would say, "If you don't know where you're going, you might wind up someplace else."[76]

Make "Kits" Sooner

For our component business, it's easy to visualize *a kit*. A kit is all of the necessary components needed to assemble a particular cabinet, like the panels, doors, drawers, accessories, and hardware. Effectively, by making the kits sooner in the process, you'll have more opportunities to catch problems before it's time to build.

This thought can be applied to nearly any process. Maybe your shop struggles with communicating information to the shop floor, which creates questions or other issues daily. If you've noticed a flood of questions, there's likely a flaw being exposed in the system that needs to be repaired. For example, in our shop the question "Where's the missing toe kick?" is a problem that's just taken someone out of their job and put them on a time-consuming hunt.

Although they can often be headaches, look at repeated questions as an opportunity to improve your systems. Once flaws are revealed, make a kit to ensure they are prevented or caught before it's time to build. If other types of issues are popping up, craft the issue into a question. If you look at a process that's linear, it's easier to look at an issue as a question.

$1, $10, $100

This one is my favorite takeaway from my talk with the retired quality process engineer. It's such a simple concept but one I'd never thought of before. Here's an example that highlights how this thought process works. Your saw man cuts parts and stacks them on a conveyor to be pushed down the line. On the last sheet, he finds a bad part that needs to be recut. Let's say the cost to do this is one dollar.

If that same part makes it to the build area when the box is partially assembled, it'll then cost $10 to fix. The reason for the 10-fold increase is that the product is near the end of the value stream. It's as close to a paycheck as it has ever been. Then you stumble onto a defective or missing part, and everything has to be stopped, reworked, and fired back up before you can continue on. This may sound exaggerated, but I assure you that every time this happens it costs the company a lot more than if it would have been caught earlier in this process.

Now, let's take the example a step further. This time instead of a missing box part, let's say it's a drawer. The job is late, and the customer is only 20 miles down the road, so the decision is made to ship it and have the service technician go fix it. Now we're looking at $100 in costs. You effectively just spent 100 times what it would have cost to fix it at the beginning.

It sounds simple, but the implications are huge. They're beyond huge, actually. They're astronomical. This is why you must push your problems and questions further uphill and away from the end of the value stream. This one point executed correctly could put your business on the fast track and ready for takeoff. Perhaps the most important point to remember in all this discussion of quality control (that will also tie into our next chapter) is this: I'm convinced that the best way to do business is to see my customers as *friends* for whom I provide a *service*. None of us would want to sell an inferior product or service to our best friend. So, doing all we can to ensure quality control is a great way to maintain friendships and build business.

Begin to practice these concepts by asking your employees every day what kind of questions they have about the production processes. Once you have a grasp on the situation, figure out how to solve these issues sooner in the process. Quality improvements will be a by-product of this exercise, and it'll pay off in spades.

UCC provides high-quality cabinet box components by following the practices in this chapter. How do you control quality with your processes?

Here's a sample quality control chart showing the process step by step.

Search for quality management software on the Capterra site for computer programs you might want to purchase to improve your company's quality control.

CHAPTER CHECKLIST

1. Have you ever purposely solicited customer feedback with the intention of using that feedback to improve either your production process or to improve customer service?

2. If you haven't done so yet, try to get at least five customer reviews as quickly as you can, and don't just cherry-pick the good ones! Get a good mix so you can make an accurate assessment of where you're starting from.

3. Do you have a process to help you catch and fix small mistakes before they grow into bigger, more costly mistakes—or even full-blown crises?

4. It is my belief that you must push your problems and questions further uphill and away from the end of the value stream. How will you put the theory into practice?

ACTION ITEM: Read number two again above and get started.

CHAPTER 12

SALES, SERVICE... SYNONYMOUS?

The key to business is personal relationships.
——Dicky Fox, *Jerry Maguire*[77]

I FIRMLY BELIEVE that when businesspeople delineate between the sales of goods and services, they risk making a crucial error. Sure, I understand that some businesses—mine included—sell products such as cars, appliances, furniture, or custom cabinets, while others sell services such as legal representation, transportation, or book publishing. But any company that fails to provide good service fails, whether their primary products are goods or services. If you've ever heard of Yogi Berra, you're probably thinking the line above sounds like a "Yogism." I suppose this is true, and that's good because we'll learn a lot from Yogi a bit later.

Patrons as Pals

If, as a business owner, I were to see my customers as nothing more than folks willing to exchange their money for my goods, I probably wouldn't have succeeded. I'm convinced that the best way to do business is to see my customers as friends for whom I provide a service. In my case, that service comes in the form of cabinets.

Here's an example of how I think about it. Mr. and Mrs. Jones have lived in their modest suburban home for decades. As they worked day after day throughout those decades, gradually their kitchen cabinets became worn and dingy. Mr. and Mrs. Jones know it's time to replace those cabinets, and they want the best product they can get for their hard-earned money. But their hard-earned money is not limitless. If I can provide a truly high-quality product that meets their needs and their style preferences at a price within their budget, then I could provide some good folks a valuable service while making a sale.

So, while I might not ever even meet Mr. and Mrs. Jones, I still want to think of them and every other customer who does business with UCC as close friends. If I were doing business with my best friend, I'd do everything possible to provide him a high-quality product at a reasonable price and to get it to him on time, undamaged, and with a smile.

Loyal Listeners Make Stellar Sellers

A key selling tip I've learned is knowing and providing precisely what your potential customers want, and the only way to know is to listen to them. Listening might seem so natural that no one needs any training on the topic. This assumption is wrong, and if your salespeople simply assume they're good listeners, they could be losing rather than gaining business for you. Here are some tips to help your salespeople improve their listening skills:

1. *Remove distractions*: Although this action is not always flawlessly feasible, a listener needs to shut out external diversions. Find a quiet place to converse with the potential client. Eliminate not only the external distractions but also the internal ones. Have you ever been talking to someone and noticed that the person's mind was elsewhere? When that happens, you probably feel like walking away—and perhaps do so. No one wants to watch his or her words metaphorically float off into space after bumping up against a pair of inattentive ears.

2. *Rehearse reserve*: Learn to set aside the natural human inclination to respond before the speaker finishes his or her thought. Real listening requires discipline, and discipline usually requires practice. Ask a friend to speak to you while you stifle your desire to respond, and instead *just listen*.

3. *Learn how to interpret*: People speak with more than just words. Various tones of voice can add nuance to the words spoken—so can gestures and body positioning. Articles like "A Beginner's Guide to Reading Body Language" by Healthline Media[78] can be a good place to start learning how to interpret these subtle signs.

4. *Be concerned*: Showing concern for the speaker's words puts you on the same page and helps build a relationship. And remember, as Dicky Fox said in the *Jerry Maguire* movie, "The key to business is personal relationships."[79]

My First Salesperson

With all the above considerations in mind, my company reached a point at which it seemed wise to hire a salesperson—preferably one who shared the philosophy outlined above. I no longer had the time to fill that role and was moving along toward the goal of firing myself. I must admit that I felt a bit of apprehension about that next step. But, finally, I began to let it be known within the local community and within the woodworking industry that I was considering hiring a salesperson.

Before long, I received a call from a woman who seemed to have the right experience and temperament for the position. Even so, I continued to wrestle with the aforementioned apprehension. What if she's not the right person? What if she's not able to bring in enough new business to justify her hiring? Or, conversely, what if she brings in more new business than we can keep up with?

After a few weeks, I overruled those wary what-ifs and hired her. The result was a good, steady growth in sales, which in turn brought the need for more production workers. As we continued to expand the production processes, it became clear that we needed more than one salesperson. We now have five full-time and one part-time salespersons who bring in more business than I could have imagined.

My Advice for Sales and Growth

My advice for growth is as follows:

1. Commit to a service-first philosophy as the foundation of your business.

2. Hire qualified employees who agree with that service-first philosophy.

3. Recognize when your business has outgrown your ability to be the sole salesperson.

4. Begin your search for a skilled and experienced salesperson who shares your service-first philosophy.

5. When you find the right person, don't hesitate to make the hire.

6. Hire more service-first production employees as needed to keep pace with increased sales.

7. Provide ongoing training for your sales team. That's a formula for achieving your goal of firing yourself.

It's also important to acknowledge that in an imperfect world populated by imperfect people even the best employees can at times find themselves working at cross purposes—or at least, not on the same page. For example, it's possible for the sales team to get too far out ahead of the production team. The obvious result of that scenario is the likelihood of being unable to deliver the products on schedule.

Communication Is the Cooperation Key

To improve communication in the shop and keep the team on the same page, here are a few things I recommend:

1. I'd advise holding regular all-staff meetings quarterly (at a minimum) to discuss interdepartmental coordination. Items to consider could include

a. an ongoing commitment to the service-first philosophy,

b. citing instances of service-first wins. Highlight examples in which following the service-first philosophy resulted in customer praise and reinforced customer relationships, and

c. honestly admitting to instances when interdepartmental communication broke down, resulting in failures to deliver products on time. Then devise and publish plans (including SOPs as needed) to resolve such issues.

2. Hold monthly or even weekly informal meetings between department heads to ensure ongoing sales and production coordination.

3. Consider publishing a monthly company newsletter aimed at fostering interdepartmental coordination and cooperation.

Conclusion: Stellar Service Sells

Most of us already instinctively know that good service keeps customers happy, and happy customers drive sales, while dissatisfied customers are likely to reduce sales. Emma Martins quantified the impact of customer service in an article on the FM Outsource website:

- When customers are happy, they have a lifetime value that's six times higher than regular customers.

- By making your customers happy, they're five times as likely to be repeat buyers and four times as likely to offer a referral to others.

- After having a positive experience, 83% of people are willing to offer a referral.

- Repeat purchasing and loyalty among a customer base can increase incremental growth by up to 20%.

- On the flip side, bad customer service leads to 95% of those customers telling others about their negative experience.[80]

There's little doubt that any company that fails to provide good service fails, whether their primary products are goods or services. That's not exactly a Yogism, but it is a Finneyism worth remembering.

CHAPTER CHECKLIST

1. Making a strong delineation between the sales of goods and services can be a crucial error. What will you do to ensure that your company never makes that potential error?

2. Do you see it as practical or impractical to view each of your customers as family members or close friends?

3. What is your assessment of your listening skills? How would family members, friends, or coworkers describe your listening habits?

4. What traits will you look for when you hire your first salesperson?

5. In your own words, how would you define a service-first philosophy?

6. What steps will you take to establish or improve interdepartmental communication at your company?

ACTION ITEM: Set a date and an agenda for an all-staff meeting where you will celebrate service-first wins and discuss even more service-first ideas.

CHAPTER 13

DRUNK ON FIVE-DOLLAR DONUTS

The consumer is not a moron; she's your wife.
—David Ogilvy[81]

HAVE YOU EVER had a five-dollar donut? Until this past summer, I'd never even heard of such a thing. My family went on a three-week tour of the West Coast, traveling through several states including California—the home of the now-infamous five-dollar donut from Sidecar Donuts.

The morning that my wife said we were going to get donuts was obviously a great morning because *who* doesn't like donuts, right? What she failed to tell me was that the donuts were crazy expensive. I'm sure this was by design so that she wouldn't have to hear me fuss about the audacity of a business charging five dollars for a single donut. Well played, woman.

The Lead-Up

Prior to our road trip, my wife laid out several stops that included the Grand Canyon, beaches in Los Angeles, San Francisco, major league baseball games, and of course, our five-dollar donuts. During her research for the trip, she'd found a local donut shop that had rave reviews, a busy Instagram page, and an overall great social presence—all the makings of a great customer experience. Their social posts not only showed the product, but they also showed them selling out with lines out the door and customers with crumb- and cream-smudged, beaming faces. Branding geniuses!

The Morning Of

My wife was really excited about this donut place, having talked about it nonstop for a couple days. To be honest, I was prepared for a letdown. It's hard to live up to that kind of hype. We planned to hit the donut shop midmorning, hopefully after their initial rush but before they ran out. Here we come, five-dollar donuts!

Arrival

Before continuing, I want to highlight a key difference in the experience of your local donut shop versus the five-dollar donut shop. I never get excited about my local donut shop. In fact, I don't look forward to it one bit. This California shop was obviously different. We were excited to go get a donut that we'd have to wait in line for. Makes perfect sense, right?

Upon arrival at Sidecar Donuts, the parking lot was completely full. Not one space was available. My blood pressure started to rise as I saw the line out the door, as I'm the type of person who's all about efficiency. Get in, get out, and get on with life. But by this point, we were committed, so I found an off-site space to park, and we followed our noses toward the intoxicating aromas.

I tried to contain my impatient sighs once we arrived in the very impressive line and kept busy by studying the daily menu on the chalkboard beside the door. Yes, my distance vision is pretty good. Between the people, I saw several unique flavors of donuts and a price of *five dollars—for each one!* I looked at my wife and said, "Five dollars?" in a quiet voice. You know the one—the whisper you wish was a shout.

But as we waited, my thoughts progressed from being slightly upset to "if they have the audacity to charge five dollars, then it must be one heck of a donut." By this point, I'd bought in and had to see this thing through. I was an eager passenger on the five-dollar donut train, expecting the porter to produce a prodigious product certain to please.

Chow Time

We all chose different donuts so that we could pass them around and experience the variety. I couldn't wait to bite into one of these amazingly aromatic confections. Once the first bite was down the hatch, I was sold! No longer was I concerned that I'd just dished out $25 for five donuts, partly because I was donut drunk.

Thirty seconds later, we'd all finished our donuts, and I was almost giddy. Why? Yes, it was a great-tasting donut but even more so because I'd been taken completely through the "buyer's journey," and now I was a raving fan. From social media and the buzz they created by having a premium-but-limited product to the great-tasting donuts and execution at the store, Sidecar Donuts nailed it.

Most businesses try to create that exceptional experience for customers, but few deliver like that five-dollar donut did. The question is how could you make your product, brand, and marketing more like the five-dollar donut and take your business to the next level on a limited budget?

How to Market on a Low Budget

"If you don't understand who you are and why you do what you do, and if you don't understand who your customer is and why they should be buying from you, then you have no business making a marketing plan."[82] That nugget of marketing advice comes from my friend Khalil Benalioulhaj, founder of Benali Marketing, a marketing agency for small businesses.

The remainder of this chapter is drawn from a three-part series Khalil taught in 2018 on my *Push Thru* podcast.

Here are some of the steps I discussed with Khalil that can help to build the personal foundation needed to achieve success:

- *Self-awareness*: More than just a vague awareness of your company's history, you need to clearly identify what your business is and why it exists. As Khalil said on my podcast, "If I were going on a date and I knew everything about the other person, but little to nothing about myself, that person is not going to want to be in a relationship with me. I have to know everything about my own company before I can reach out to the customers I'm trying to target." He went on to explain that every business needs to connect with its *why*. Once the *why* is solidified for you, it is much easier to communicate your company's unique spot in the marketplace. "When customers understand why you do what you do, that's when they really want to buy from you."[83] Note: If you're confused, revisit chapter two, when we looked at developing your company's vision statement. Keep it short and to the point but with big implications.

- *Product awareness*: Not unlike the business owner, each product or service the company offers has its own origin and purpose. As Khalil said, "Once people understand what that product is and why it exists, it doesn't matter what the technical specifications are; they just want to know the purpose and meaning of it and how it's attached to your company's purpose. ... So, questions to ask yourself then are:

  » Why does this product or service exist?

  » Why do we offer it?

  » How can we communicate that to people so that they can clearly understand why the product exists?

  » Why do customers need this product?

  » Why should they choose this product over competitors' offerings?

  » How does the product benefit our customers?

  » How does the product work?

  » How is it delivered?"[84]

THAT'S IT I'M FIRED!

- *The story plus the product*: Some products—like those blissful five-dollar donuts—are so unique and appealing at a primal level that people will stand in long lines to savor the mind-blowing taste. But no one's likely to start salivating at the thought of a top-notch cabinet. I need to help sell my products by selling my story.

- *Customer awareness*: Now we'll connect the business persona to the customer persona. For example, I'm a middle-aged man who produces and markets cabinets and cabinet components. That's likely to be a yawner for Gen Z and even for those at the younger end of Gen Y, most of whom don't yet own homes. Instead, my audience is far more likely to be baby boomers and Gen Xers, folks closer to my age. I already have a bit of an advantage since I'm likely to be selling to my contemporaries. Our stories are likely to be at least somewhat similar. But to seal the deal, I need to sell my story as their story. In doing so, I create a bond. If my products were computer games, I'd probably need to have a Gen Z partner whose story more closely matched that of our potential customers. The next step is to assess the particulars of this demographic:

  » Are they married?

  » Do they have children in the home?

  » Renters or homeowners?

  » Hobbies?

  » Educational background?

  » Information sources?

The more you know about your customers, the better you'll be at making a connection with them.

Another important point to consider regarding customer awareness is whether the target customers are B2B or B2C. Understanding the lives and stories of other businesses is not the same as understanding the stories of direct individual customers. We'll expand on this point and several others later.

CHAPTER CHECKLIST

1. Have you ever eaten a donut—or a steak or a slice of apple pie—that was so mouthwatering that you'd stand in a long line and pay almost any price to experience it again? If your product or service is not that inherently "tasty," what can you do to build a level of anticipation about it?

2. Socrates said, "To know thyself is the beginning of wisdom."[85] Khalil Benalioulhaj says the first step in marketing your business should be self-awareness; know yourself. Do you agree? If so, take a moment to describe yourself.

3. Like the business owner, each product or service the company offers has its own story—its origin and purpose. Do you know the story of each of your products or services?

4. Have you identified the likely demographic of your customers? If so, how much do you know about them?

ACTION ITEM: Write out what you know about the likely demographic of your customers.

CHAPTER 14

MARKETING: CREATING A GROWTH PLAN

The idea of a growth plan is to intentionally plot out the steps that you need to take in order to achieve the growth you desire.

—Khalil Benalioulhaj, Benali Marketing[86]

IN THE PREVIOUS chapter, along with Khalil Benalioulhaj, we looked at building a foundation for marketing through self-awareness, product awareness, and customer awareness. Now we'll look at where to go after the foundation is built.

Determine Priorities

The growth plan is not an end but rather a means to achieve even bigger goals and form greater priorities. Remember, way back in chapter one we saw my business coach, Martin Holland, ask his clients a very basic question: "What do you want?" The question seems so simple one wonders why it needs to be asked. But, surprisingly, it's not that uncommon for people to set out on a journey, head off to college, or begin a business, without first establishing exactly where they want to end up. So, before we establish the particulars of our growth plan, we need to determine our priorities.

Keep in mind too that most of us do have several priorities, and they can be difficult to tackle effectively and efficiently at once. Khalil suggests focusing on no more than three at a time, and even then, one should take precedence over the others.

Set Goals to Achieve Priorities

If your priorities are big, so will be the goals set to reach them. Since grand goals can appear daunting to the point of being discouraging, Khalil suggests breaking those goals down into smaller pieces. For example, he recommends that "if your grand goal is to gain 12 new clients for the year, then don't look at it as 12 for the year, but rather as one per month, or three per quarter."[87]

The question is, when setting those goals aimed at the big-picture priorities, should we shoot for the stars, knowing they'll almost certainly remain out of reach? Or should we set goals that require some stretching but that we can be confident of attaining? The answer to this question is you must consider the personalities of your team members as you set those goals. Some members might be discouraged to the point of surrender if given lofty goals. Others, however, might coast if their goals seem too easily attained. The bottom line is that people are motivated differently. It's important for a boss to know his or her team members well enough to provide the correct motivation for each person.

Setting the Revenue Goal

Khalil advises this: "What [products or services] make up the majority of your sales? From there, how much of those product or service sales does it take to reach that revenue mark that you set? ... Then, if you're aiming for $100,000 in sales, and the top products sell for $10,000 each, then we need to make 10 sales to reach our revenue goal."[88] This way, we're not focusing daily on the revenue but instead focusing on the products or services. That advice might sound overly simple, but sometimes we need simplicity for the sake of clarity. Sometimes, in a rushed business world, we can't see the forest of our long-term goals for the trees of rushed daily demands.

In order to know where you're going, you need to know where you are now. Track the metrics that matter. A good way to gauge your sales metrics is through a sales funnel.

The Sales Funnel

There are various versions of a sales funnel. Khalil's version is below: Where are we currently? How many prospects? How many leads? How many qualified leads? How many opportunities? How many customers? Start measuring those metrics now. This will allow you to measure results.

If we're selling 20 products per month now and we want to be selling 40 per month, then we probably need to double the number at each stage all the way back to the top. In other words, if it takes 500 prospects to yield 300 leads, and 300 leads to yield 100 qualified leads, and 100 qualified leads to yield 50 opportunities, and 50 opportunities to yield 20 customers, then to get to 40 customers we need to start with 1,000 prospects. If that sounds daunting, don't worry, we'll cover it in more detail in the next chapter.

The next step is to look for ways to improve success at each level of the funnel. Perhaps the sales process can become more efficient and allow you to gain more than 100 qualified leads from 300 leads. Plenty of apps and software programs are available to improve efficiencies at various levels of the sales and growth processes. Software Advice lists scores of programs along these lines.

Use Your Uniqueness

It's important to tailor your marketing strategy to your unique business. Khalil says, "Perhaps, this quarter it's more important to focus on follow-ups. Perhaps it's we don't need more marketing; we need more referrals. ... Do you ask for referrals? If you don't, and you're getting referrals without asking, what would happen if you did ask for them? What would happen if you created a referral program where you rewarded someone with a discount or a gift card if they do give you a referral?"[89]

Or perhaps business reviews provide a huge boost. One way to get more customer reviews is to call those clients and arrange a process for soliciting those customer reviews.

Metrics, Meet Goals

Once you've determined your goals and analyzed your metrics, you must determine how to drive those metrics to meet the goals. Start by establishing the steps needed and then assign people to be responsible for each step—it's that simple. And one of the first things you can do to push those metrics toward your goals is to maximize the use of your website.

If your company doesn't have a website, you'll need to create one as soon as possible to remain competitive. Fortunately, there are affordable options that will allow you to build your own using programs like Wordpress or Wix. If you have no experience in doing so, I'd suggest hiring a professional website designer. These 10 top website design services listed by Quick Sprout can be helpful if you need a little help getting started.[90]

According to an article on The Blueprint, these are the things you need to consider as you design and build your small-business website:

- What is the main purpose of your website?

- What is your brand identity?

- What is your budget?

To learn more, check out "7 Simple Steps to Create a Website for Your Small Business."[91]

CHAPTER CHECKLIST

1. What are your priorities? Have you established them yet?

2. How will you break down your priorities into smaller, more manageable goals?

3. Remember to consider the personalities of your team members as you set those goals.

4. Do you have a company website? If not, why not? If so, how are you using it? How can you use it to generate more leads?

ACTION ITEM: If you don't have a company website, get started now. Go to the article listed above, "7 Simple Steps to Create a Website for Your Small Business," and move your business into the twenty-first century. If you do have a company website, review it against the info provided by the article above. Is it on the mark?

CHAPTER 15

INTRO TO INBOUND MARKETING

The best marketing doesn't feel like marketing.
—Tom Fishburne[92]

"IT'S ALL ABOUT education, equipping, and empowering."[93] That's how our friend and marketing adviser Khalil Benalioulhaj summarizes inbound marketing, the next step in our growth strategy. Let's look at each of the three elements of inbound marketing.

Education

Maybe you know you have a great product or service, but how much do your current and potential customers know about your products or services? Do they know what makes those products special and what differentiates them from your competitors' products? Beyond that, can you go the extra mile to help those potential customers learn more about the industry you represent? In doing so, you present yourself as an expert on the topic, and a potential customer will feel more comfortable doing business with a topic expert. (Note: Obviously, if you present yourself as a topic expert, you'd better be just that. If you lack expertise, you'll set yourself up for failure and ridicule.)

The next step is to understand and address the needs of potential customers. To do this, you should be able to demonstrate how your product answers those needs. When doing this, be specific. *Here* (in detail) *is how my product (or service) addresses your needs, performs the required task, or scratches your itch.* "Education," Khalil says, "is letting those potential customers know everything they need to know about you, your company, and the industry."[94]

Equipping

"Equipping is just giving your customers the tools and resources they need, whatever helps them accomplish their goals," Khalil says. "What's an example of a tool a seller might provide to a buyer? I can give my customers knowledge about marketing all day long, but if they don't have the tools to execute on their marketing, then they're not going to make a lot of progress. So, if [my client] is trying to write a blog post, then I need to provide them a template that will help them craft the post in an efficient and effective manner."[95] This element ties back to the self-awareness, product awareness, and customer awareness we outlined in chapter 12. If you know who you are (individually and corporately), what you have to offer, and what the customer needs, then you're ready to equip your customer when they express their needs.

Empowering

This element is all about customer service. Remember, back in chapter 11 we discussed that a company fails when good customer service isn't provided, whether their primary products are goods or services. This means going the extra mile. For instance, perhaps the product you sold had a one-year warranty, but it's been closer to two years since you sold it to them. When the customer calls to tell you that the product isn't working properly, rather than brush them off with a reminder to look at the warranty's expiration date, you listen to the customer's concern.

If the item was relatively inexpensive, it might be worth your while to consider replacing it at no cost. If the product was more costly, it could prove profitable in the long term to go have a look at the product, assess the problem, and determine if it can be repaired. If not, you might consider offering a replacement at a dramatically reduced cost. Keeping an ongoing customer and turning that customer into a satisfied ambassador for your company is well worth the cost of replacing or repairing a problematic product.

Why Is Inbound Marketing So Effective?

"Inbound marketing is about reaching today's marketplace," Khalil says. "Yesterday's pre-internet marketplace was a seller's market. The sellers had all the information. In order to get that information, buyers had to seek out the seller to get that information before making a purchase decision. A great example of this is the auto industry. Twenty years ago, if you were going to buy a car, you had to visit every dealership in the area and talk to several salespeople. And then you weren't sure who to trust. Is this a good deal? At the end of the day—or days—you had to make a decision based on this lengthy research process or just take the first offer and hope for the best."[96]

That auto shopping experience has completely changed. Now a car shopper can learn everything he or she needs to know without ever leaving home, as all the decision-making information is available on the internet. Now the buyers have all the information and the accompanying power. In the old days, cash was king. In today's marketplace, content is king. "If you can start building content," Khalil says, "then you'll do better than your competitors."[97] Those potential customers are doing their internet research, so you need to be the one they find, the one who answers their questions and provides the product they need.

The Buyer's Journey

According to HubSpot, the buyer's journey consists of three phases: *awareness, consideration,* and *decision.*[98]

- *Awareness:* "Buyers are identifying the challenge or opportunity they want to pursue." The potential customer realizes he or she is facing either a problem or an opportunity.

- *Consideration:* "Buyers have clearly defined the goal or challenge and have committed to addressing it. They are now evaluating different approaches or methods available to pursue the goal or solve their challenge."

- *Decision*: Now the customer knows what he or she wants. Where do I shop for it? These days, most folks will begin their shopping phase with internet research. If you're not doing inbound marketing, those potential customers are not likely to ever come across your company and your products.

As a business owner, my job is to answer each of the questions for each of the three phases listed above. If I already have content created that helps them through those phases, I'm walking them down the path to my door. And by the time they reach the decision phase, they're already there, waiting for me to welcome them in.

Getting Started with Inbound Marketing

In chapter 12, we looked at customer awareness, knowing who your potential customers are, as well as their needs and goals. From there, we made a list of questions based on old emails from customers. Why? Because if your past and current customers have asked these questions, it's likely that future customers will have the same questions. Now you're ready to answer those questions without spending time looking them up. In addition, ask your employees to pass along to you the questions customers asked them.

As you answer those questions, you're creating content for inbound marketing and can publish them on your website, blogs, and other social media. You can also record answers to questions and post the video to sites like YouTube or hold live workshops. Publishing choices depend largely on your customer awareness findings. Where do your customers get their information? Once you can answer that question, you'll know where to meet them for your inbound marketing.

The next question is, how do you capture the leads generated through those blog posts, social media sites, and workshops? Again, the top spot is your own website, and that website needs to be structured in a manner that collects leads effectively. Yes, a contact form, but you should also have a sign-up for a newsletter and a way for customers to schedule a product demonstration. Then, every publicity component you produce should direct those potential customers to those capture portals. This will allow your website to have everything the potential customer needs throughout buyer's cycle. If your website doesn't answer all the buyer's questions, they'll likely move on to another site that does.

One more point that should be made here is that all this information distribution must be free. Think of it as establishing an initial relationship, and after the buyer has seen the value of the information provided, they'll be more likely to want to hear your sales pitch.

Remember that if a potential customer is overwhelmingly pleased with the information you've provided, they'll remember you when it's time to make a purchase and be more likely to tell others about you as well.

CHAPTER CHECKLIST

1. How much do your customers and potential customers know about your products or services?

2.   Are you equipped to present yourself as an expert on your topic? If not, what will you do to become that expert?

3.   Are you certain that you understand the needs of your potential customers? If you do, then take a moment to write out your understanding of those needs. If not, begin your research.

4.   What tools and resources do you have that will help your potential customers accomplish their goals?

5.   What lengths are you willing to go to in order to make a satisfied ambassador for your company?

6.   Understanding that potential customers are doing their internet research, what are you doing to ensure you're the one they find?

7.   What are you doing to create great content for inbound marketing?

ACTION ITEM: Question two above asks if you're equipped to present yourself as an expert on your topic. If you aren't certain that you're an expert, start researching. As you do so, take notes of new things you learn.

CHAPTER 16:

IGNORANCE IS NOT BLISS

In theory, there is no difference
between theory and practice. In practice, there is.
—Benjamin Brewster[99]

MY EMPLOYEES ARE proud of the work they do, and I'm proud of them for taking the time to learn how to do their work effectively and efficiently. Most of them would candidly admit that they have little to no training in business, finance, or economics. Nor are they inclined to seek such training, as they truly enjoy production work. If they'd wanted to own a company of their own, they'd have pursued that goal.

My production employees tend to be Type C and D personalities. As you might recall from chapter six, Type C folks tend to be logical, detail oriented, and dependable. Type D tend to be task oriented and stable but also cautious. The business world needs Type A personalities like me who want a greater degree of autonomy and who are willing to take big risks to gain that sense of sovereignty. But businesses cannot run properly without other personality types, like Cs and Ds.

The Practical Side of the Theories of Practices

It's likely that most production workers, regardless of their personality type, are happy to leave the financial factors and economic equations to Type A personalities who spend most of their time in offices analyzing sales figures and seeking paths to better profit ratios. However, I've learned that providing those non–Type A production workers some education and insight into the company's economic big picture benefits them individually and all of us corporately. My education came partially through simple observations but also from a book I read titled *The Great Game of Business* by Jack Stack.[100] That book flipped my perspective on company communications in general and, more specifically, on communicating with employees about the company's finances.

After I read the book, I tried something new at our annual company Christmas party. I had all the employees sit far enough apart that they couldn't see what others would write. Then I gave them all paper and pens and asked them to write down anonymously their guess as to what our company's top-line sales figures were. Next, I had them write down their guess as to the company's bottom line, after paying *all* expenses, including their salaries, wages, benefits, and all other forms of compensation.

That year, our top-line sales were about $1.5 million. The employees' guesses ranged from $100,000 to $700,000. In other words, far below actual sales. When I gave them our actual sales numbers, they were shocked—and impressed. When it came to the bottom-line profits, the guesses ranged from $80,000 to $500,000, versus an actual figure of about $150,000.

Clearly, many of my employees had little to no idea of our company's actual sales or profits (I'll explain why this could be a big problem shortly). It was clear I needed to provide some education. The next time we met corporately, we played the profit game. On a long piece of construction paper, I wrote the word "Sales," then "Cost of Goods Sold," then "Expenses," and finally, at the bottom, "Net Profit." Prior to the meeting, I'd bought fake money and divided it into bundles of $50,000. I had the sales team place $1.5 million on the top line next to "Sales." Next, I had our engineer put the equivalent in phony money of what we spent on "Cost of Goods Sold." The shop floor employees placed the dollars for "Labor" on the "Expenses" line—and then I added to that all the other smaller expenses. After deducting the cost of goods sold and the expenses from the top-line sales, they could see in a more tangible portrayal the dramatic difference between sales and profits.

Why Does It Matter? Allies, Not Foes

"Why go to all that trouble?" you might ask. As I see it, by imparting this knowledge (sometimes referred to as *open-book management*), we business owners gain in at least the following four ways:

- *It instills a sense of pride of accomplishment* (personal and team). That a small niche business like ours, operating in a relatively small market, can generate annual sales of more than $1.5 million makes every person on the team feel good. And although our ultimate goal is not to generate good feelings, doing so is not a meaningless accomplishment. It provides a sense of personal value and is good for company productivity at the same time.

- *It can also help to build team unity, which obviously benefits the entire team.* It's easy to see that high productivity requires each team member to perform his or her duty effectively and efficiently. *If I slack off, the entire team is negatively affected. If I perform at a high level, the entire team prospers.* Success for the team depends on the efforts and success of every one of the individuals.

- *It helps each team member to understand that the owner is their ally, not their foe.* When employees see that the vast majority of the sales income goes to business expenses—and that the largest of those expenses is employee pay and benefits—they're more likely to see the business owner as their ally rather than as a foe who seeks to exploit them as he or she lives a lavish lifestyle. Of course, this assumes you, the business owner, really are pulling with your employees rather than exploiting them. If that's not the case, I'd suggest you go back and start reading this book again, from the beginning of chapter one.

- *It can improve employee retention.* In chapter four, we looked at the high cost of employee turnover and, conversely, the savings and profitability of employee retention. An employee who is concerned about his employer's financial stability is more likely to search out other employment opportunities than an employee who perceives the company's financial situation as secure. Obviously for this to be true, your company needs to be in a secure financial state.

"We're Lost, but We're Making Good Time."[101]

Yes, that subtitle above is another Yogi Berra aphorism. Yogi was a genius at making himself appear ignorant. Ignorance can be funny, in certain situations. But it can also be harmful and dangerous. Regarding your business, having ignorant employees is not a plus. Your employees will gain from being given more information, and that includes financial information.

So, the next obvious question—the one you're no doubt asking right now—is, What kind of financial information should I divulge to my employees? In "4 Things All Employees Should Know about Financial Analysis," an article appearing on Andromeda Simulations International's website, the authors saw the following four elements as essential for employees' education:

1. "They should know the common language...Without a common language, effective teamwork is nearly impossible."

2. "They should know how their decisions contribute to results...Every action by every employee matters."

3. "They should know that profit is not the same as cash. ... Just because they [employees] contribute to a profitable

sale doesn't necessarily mean the company is better for it in the immediate future."

4. "They should know that timing is everything. ... Understanding the relationship between time and cash flow will inform decisions made at every level of a company."[102]

Not surprising to me was that much within the Andromeda Simulations International article was drawn from an article titled "Ten Rules for Great Finance" by Ari Weinzweig,[103] who in turn credited many of his ideas to *The Great Game of Business* by Jack Stack, the book I referred to earlier in this chapter. Are you beginning to see the value in reading Stack's book when you finish this one? A successful entrepreneur never stops observing, learning, or imparting useful knowledge to his or her employees.

And as the great Yogi Berra once said, "You can observe a lot by just watching."[104]

CHAPTER CHECKLIST

1. As a business owner, you're probably like me in being a Type A personality. But, as I wrote above, businesses cannot run properly without other personality types like Cs and Ds. Have you begun yet to look at personality-type tests for your employees?

2. What kind of responses would you expect from your employees if you asked them about your company's top-line and bottom-line finances?

3. If the replies to that question made you concerned, what will you do to educate your employees?

4. Of the four things I listed as important elements of employee knowledge, which do you see as most important?

5. How will you go about keeping your employees regularly updated on your company's financial situation?

6. Bottom line: Don't put yourself in the position of having to confess, as Yogi Berra once did, "We made too many wrong mistakes."[105]

ACTION ITEM: Write out your plan for keeping your employees regularly updated on your company's financial situation.

CHAPTER 17

PRACTICALLY POSITIVE

Doing what you love is the cornerstone of having
abundance in your life.
—Wayne Dyer

PLEASE DON'T ASSUME I'm some Pollyanna-ish, unremitting, unrealistic optimist. Although I am an optimist, I'm also a realist. I understand that we live in a world that has limits. For instance, the planet's potable water could potentially run out. But when we develop an efficient, cost-effective means for large-scale desalination of ocean water, that limit will suddenly become *nearly* limitless.

I'm optimistic about that development occurring soon, as evidenced in this statement from Keiken Engineering. "Reverse Osmosis one of the best options for desalination of the seawater.

It is [a] highly effective, cost-effective, and safe option that can save a lot of time and effort. It comes with a wide range of benefits and advantages, making it an efficient system for desalination."[106]

Early in my business career, I operated under the common mindset that both supplies and consumers are limited. Granted, that's technically true. The number of trees on the planet is finite, and so is the number of human beings. But when you look at the real numbers, they do seem *almost* limitless. Currently, Earth is home to more than three trillion trees[107] and nearly eight billion humans.[108] That's a number most of us cannot truly comprehend. To add to this fact, a conservative figure states that the average 19-inch diameter tree contains about 300-board feet of lumber.[109]

So that means that right now this world is home to 9 x 10 to the 14th power of potential board feet of lumber. That's a number so high we have no simple name for it. It's almost like the number of grains of sand on the planet's beaches. Theoretically, it would be possible to count all those grains of sand and one day find the last one.

Mind you, I'm not suggesting that humans should rush out and harvest all or most of the lumber from the planet's three trillion trees. I'm merely pointing out the vastness of our world's resources. And don't forget, trees are a renewable resource. As mature trees are harvested, more are being planted. When it comes to potential customers, consider this: The United States has a net gain of one new person every 40 seconds.[110] In the time it would take the average reader to read this book straight through to this point, the United States would gain about 114 more people.

Attitude Accelerates Attainment

When you, your new salesperson, or your entire skilled sales team hits the road, dials the phone, or sends that promotional mailing, do so with a mindset of abundance rather than of scarcity. Wayne Dyer is right: "Abundance is not something we acquire. It is something we tune into."

In "3 Ways to Achieve a Winning Sales Attitude," Colleen Stanley cites a Met Life Insurance study that made a significant discovery. "Salespeople who scored high in optimism sold 33% more insurance than those who scored lower. After two years, these optimistic salespeople were thriving in their positions. Turnover decreased and sales increased because Met Life focused on hiring for optimism, not just hard selling skills."[111] Are your sales employees pessimists or optimists? When they look out at the world and their potential customers specifically, do they see scarcity or abundance? Do they see one lightning-struck, diseased, gnarled old oak, or do they see three trillion thriving trees? Do they only see the one potential customer who snarled a snarky no? Or do they see 330 million other Americans, each of whom might be in the market for the product or service their company can provide them?

A Tale of Two Travelers

No one seems to know the origin of the following story that wonderfully illustrates the difference between pessimism and optimism, but it's worth reading for the first time or rereading for the 10th time:

There was once a traveler who was walking from a village in the mountains to a village in the valley. As he walked along, he saw a monk working in a field, so he stopped and said to the monk, "I'm on my way to the village in the valley. Can you tell me what it's like?"

The monk looked up from his labor and asked the man where he had come from.

The man responded, "I have come from the village in the mountains."

"What was that like?" the monk asked.

"Terrible!" the man exclaimed. "No one spoke my language, I had to sleep on a dirt floor in one of their houses, they fed me some sort of stew that had yak or dog or both in it, and the weather was atrocious."

"Then I think that you will find that the village in the valley is much the same," the monk noted.

A few hours later another traveler passed by, and he said to the monk, "I am on my way to the village in the valley. Can you tell me what it's like?"

"Where have you come from?" inquired the monk.

"I have come from the village in the mountains."

"And what was that like?"

"It was awesome!" the man replied. "No one spoke my language, so we had to communicate using our hands and facial expressions. I had to sleep on the dirt floor, which was cool as I've never done that before. They fed me some sort of weird stew, and I have no

idea what was in it, but just to experience how the locals lived was great, and the weather was freezing cold, which meant that I really got a taste of the local conditions. It was one of the best experiences of my life."

"Then I think that you'll find that the village in the valley is much the same," responded the monk.[112]

Can a Pessimist Become an Optimist?

Are you more like the first or the second traveler? Are you more of a pessimist or an optimist? If you're unsure, it might be a good idea to analyze your optimistic and pessimistic tendencies.

If you find that you tend to be pessimistic, don't despair—you can change just as I have. In his book *Learned Optimism*, psychologist Martin Seligman, who led the above-mentioned Met Life Insurance study on the effects of optimism on sales, leads readers through the process of realigning their thoughts and behaviors from pessimism to optimism.[113] I'd suggest reading Seligman's book, but until then try following these suggestions from "8 Ways to Become an Optimist."

1. Reframe those "disasters."

2. Take control.

3. Stay away from downers.

4. Pay attention to what makes you feel optimistic.

5. Reward yourself.

6. Strive for real conversations.

7. Do look at that glass as half-full.

8. Be glad.[114]

You might now be saying something like, "Without explanations, those eight directives are little more than meaningless platitudes. Why didn't he include the clarifications?" Well, the first answer to that question is copyright laws. If I'd included the authors' clarifications of each of those points, I'd have greatly exceeded fair use laws. But another reason I left them open was so that I could give you, the reader, an assignment. Before you go to the "8 Ways to Become an Optimist" page, give a shot at defining each of the eight points for yourself.

CHAPTER CHECKLIST

1. Try to imagine three trillion trees. Can't do it? Okay, try to imagine one trillion dollar bills. Far smaller than three trillion trees, right? But still a figure beyond imagination. To help imagine the scale, here's an image of an average man standing next to *one trillion dollars*:

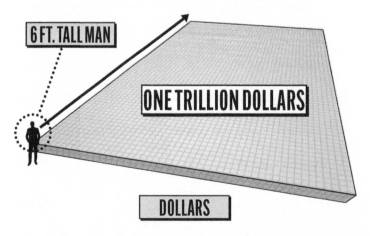

Now consider that each tree is at least one thousand times the size of a dollar bill, and we're talking about *three* trillion trees vs. *one* trillion dollars.

 x1,000

3 million trees
in the world

So, at this scale, we'd need 3,000 one-trillion-dollar grids to equal the world's trees.

That means that for full scale we'd need 864,000 one-trillion-dollar grids (of the above scale) to equal the mass of the world's trees.

I know of no way to write out a number for 864,000 times one trillion. Do you?

2. Now let's try to picture (nearly) eight billion human beings. Below is an aerial photo of a stadium crowd estimated at between 40,000 and 50,000.

In order to get high enough to get most of the crowd in the photo, the images become almost indistinct as humans. And this is just 50,000 (or perhaps slightly fewer). Eight billion is at least 160,000 times the number seen in this photo. If just one-quarter of 1 percent might be potential customers for your products or services, then you have 20 million people to reach out to. Get to work!

3. Do you think optimism is inborn or learned?

4. If it's the latter and some of your sales team members are pessimists, what will you do to help them become optimists?

ACTION ITEM: Are you or your team members pessimists? Find one or two pessimistic thoughts or beliefs you have and work to change those today.

CHAPTER 18

UPGRADE UNDERPERFORMERS—OR CUT THE CORD?

HOW TO KNOW WHEN AN EMPLOYEE IS NOT A GOOD FIT—AND WHAT TO DO ABOUT IT

There are only two kinds of employees that I've run across in 30 years. There are ones that get results, and ones that make excuses. If you're in that second camp, you're not going to like Dish.
—Charlie Ergen[115]

BEFORE I HIRE a new employee, I look first at the processes we're following. I ask myself, Do I need a new employee, or do I need to improve a process? Generally, when I see a need to add a new employee, it's usually because my business is growing and processes need to be broken down into smaller, more manageable chunks. The new hire's focus will be to tend to that new chunk, so to speak.

Until about 18 months ago, I'd never had an office manager. I'd automated as many of the processes as I could, but even so, the clerical side of the business was demanding too much of my attention. The addition proved to be a big bonus, one that easily paid for the added wage of another employee. Doing so has made us more efficient, aligning us with our vision statement, "To be the most efficient cabinet component manufacturer in the world!"

When the Line Is Crossed

On the flip side, I once promoted a man to a role he soon proved to be incapable of handling. When his inability to handle the bigger role became manifestly obvious, I knew I had no choice but to move him back to his previous position. That demotion embittered him. And despite my subsequent efforts to convince him that he was still part of the team and that we valued his work in his original role, he would not be appeased. It soon became apparent that his negative attitude was infecting the entire company culture. I had to dismiss him.

My concern was that I might have waited too long to do so and that his negative mindset might have already affected others. In time, we moved on and cleared the table. Company culture was restored, and I learned from that episode that it's just as important to protect and preserve a good company culture as it is to protect my financial assets, my reputation, or even my family. And I know

now that protecting the company's culture requires swift action to remove the cancer of a culture killer.

Watching the Early Warning Signs

It's always important to keep an eye out for bad apples. Here are a few early warning signs that I look for to see if an employee isn't functioning in the job he or she was hired to do:

1. *The person just isn't getting the work done.* The work is either not done at all, not up to standard, or late.

2. *The employee shows clear signs of disengagement.* He or she might not verbalize it, but anyone watching can see that the person is doing little more than going through the motions.

3. *The person appears to lack confidence and the necessary skills.* It could be that the person wants to do well but isn't capable of performing the required tasks.

How should a business owner deal with underperforming employees?

Remember, as we saw in chapter four, according to the Terra Staffing Group:

- It will cost $12,000 to replace an entry-level employee making $36,000 a year.

- It will cost $20,000 to replace a manager making $60,000 a year.

- It will cost $50,000 to replace an executive making $150,000 a year.[116]

These statistics point to why a wise owner doesn't take firing an employee lightly. Termination should be our last resort, and before such an extreme action, we should always look for ways to help a struggling employee improve his or her performance.

Upgrade Underperformers

Before I delve too deeply into steps for helping underperforming employees, I need to include a crucial caveat. *Don't overthink the process.* Yes, at times a boss might be responsible for an employee's poor performance, and I'll note such possibilities below. But sometimes the problem lies squarely at the dragging or disobedient feet of the poor performer.

Earlier in my entrepreneurial era, I often spent days, weeks, or even months agonizing over a decision about terminating a troublesome or underperforming employee. I finally came to realize that some people, although usually a small number, don't really want to work. People like this need to be removed quickly before their attitude and actions influence other employees.

Now let's consider how an employer can help an underperforming employee.

1. *Probe the problem*: Before a business owner begins guiding an underperforming employee, he or she needs to do some serious self-reflection: Is this employee struggling because the owner failed to clearly define the employee's duties? Or might the employee's struggles be tied to an issue in the work environment? Do they, as the boss, need to make adjustments on their end that will help their employees perform more effectively and efficiently? If this is the case,

then, obviously begin here. Correct the underlying issue that hinders employees' performances.

2. *Explain expectations*: This ties back to number one. If, as the boss, the owner failed to clearly define the employee's duties and the expectations for the job, then they need to begin by correcting their mistake of assuming too much. They need to ensure that the employee knows precisely what his or her job duties are.

3. *Assemble assessable aims*: This, obviously, is closely linked to numbers one and two. It isn't enough to verbalize to the employee his or her duties. The goals need to be recorded digitally or on paper in a place where the owner and the employee can easily review them. And, as alluded to above, those goals need to be clearly defined and measurable. Many refer to this step as a performance improvement plan.

4. *Meet methodically*: The owner and employee agreed on a set of measurable goals, so it's important to meet regularly to assess whether the goals are being met. If the employee has turned things around and is now regularly performing up to or even exceeding expectations, these meetings are the right time for praise.

Cut the Cord: Why and How

The need to remove an employee can arise for various reasons. Here are a few:

1. *The employee consistently disrupts the company's culture.* This ties back to the need for teamwork, as discussed in chapter four. No matter how productive an employee may be, if

he or she thwarts teamwork, he or she must either realign with the company's vision and mission or be replaced.

2. *The employee violates company and common cultural customs or laws.* An employee who, for example, repeatedly uses nonprescription drugs on the job despite company prohibitions cannot be allowed to continue.

3. *The employee consistently underperforms.* If, after following the measures cited above (under "Upgrade Underperformers"), the employee continues to underperform, then a prudent business owner has no choice but to consider terminating that employee.

So, upon detecting that an employee has reached one of the three points listed above, how should a small-business owner move through the termination process? What are the best steps to take to help the terminated employee improve his or her future job prospects and to avoid any legal repercussions for yourself and your company?

1. *If you have an attorney, begin the termination process by discussing it with your legal representative.* Keeping an attorney on retainer isn't inexpensive, but losing a wrongful termination case could be far more expensive. To learn more about keeping a retainer, read "How Much Is a Typical Retainer Fee for a Lawyer?" by Wylda Ivan.[117]

2. *Plan ahead for the termination meeting.* Don't wing it. This is not a time for improvisation, and the wrong words or phrases could cost you mightily. If you do have an attorney, discuss beforehand how you will conduct the termination meeting and what you'll say. Know before you

begin whether you'll provide severance pay and have your documentation ready. Here in Oklahoma, we're required to give two warnings, and on the second, you must state that a third infraction could or will result in termination.

3. *Have a witness*: It's always best to have someone to corroborate your account of the meeting should the terminated employee later try to dispute your report of the meeting.

4. *Be cordial*: This is not personal but rather a necessary business decision. You're doing what's best for your business and all your other employees and wish no ill will for the terminated employee. If you're going to give severance pay, try to have it on hand to give at the termination meeting. If not, explain to the person when and how the severance will be paid.

5. *Document the meeting*: Record the essence of the meeting. Note how you explained the termination and how the employee reacted. Keep this record with all the other records you made along the way toward the termination.

The Workest article "How to Terminate an Employee (with Sample Scripts)" provides sample scripts that can help you decide what to say at the termination meeting. And it's important to remember, as the above website article states, to be as direct as possible. "There's no point sugar-coating it: let the employee know they're being let go at the onset. If you're firing the employee for cause, you may want to briefly cover the policy violation or infractions that led to their dismissal. If you're relieving the employee of their duties at-will, you'll want to let them know that is the reason they're being terminated."[118]

Is Severance Pay Suitable?

When trying to determine suitable severance pay, keep in mind what the US Department of Labor's stance is on severance pay. "Severance pay is often granted to employees upon termination of employment. It is usually based on length of employment for which an employee is eligible upon termination. There is no requirement in the Fair Labor Standards Act for severance pay. Severance pay is a matter of agreement between an employer and an employee (or the employee's representative). The Employee Benefits Security Administration (EBSA) may be able to assist an employee who did not receive severance benefits under their employer-sponsored plan. Please contact EBSA if you have any questions."[119]

While that comes from the federal government, state laws vary. According to the *Employment Law Handbook* here in Oklahoma, "Labor laws do not require employers to provide employees with severance pay. If an employer chooses to provide severance benefits, it must comply with the terms of its established policy or employment contract."[120] Check the Employment Law Handbook for specifics on severance pay and many other labor-law issues specific to your state.

Obviously, severance pay is more likely to be given to employees who are laid off rather than to those who are terminated for ethics or performance violations.

For more information on severance pay in general terms, see Indeed's "Guide to Severance Pay."[121]

For more information on severance pay for fired employees, see Indeed's "Guide to Severance Pay for Fired Employees."[122]

CHAPTER CHECKLIST

1. Do you see any of your current employees described in the early warning signs listed in the beginning of the chapter?

2. If you do, follow the steps listed under the subheading "Upgrade Underperformers."

3. If you have not yet investigated the idea of keeping a qualified attorney on retainer, consider that possibility now.

4. If you face the prospect of firing an employee, what steps will you take?

5. Will you establish a set of guidelines for terminating employees?

6. Will you build into your budget a fund to cover severance packages?

7. Will you establish a set of guidelines for providing severance packages?

ACTION ITEM: Begin writing your set of guidelines for terminating employees.

CHAPTER 19

├───────────────────────────┤

WHEN CAN YOU FIRE YOURSELF?

Yesterday's home runs don't win today's games.
—Unknown

WELL, HERE WE are, at the crossroads. Are you fully in on firing yourself? If you are, I suspect you've already begun implementing the advice given in the previous chapters. If you aren't fully on board, beware. You might end up like a nice but insolvent old man I met a few years ago.

Yes, a few years ago I attended an auction at a retiring woodworker's shop. The kind old man had spent his life working hard to make a good living, yet all his hard work didn't add up to much when he reached retirement age. When the dust settled, the auction brought in about $45,000. While that's a nice chunk of money, I can imagine it wasn't enough to fund the man's retirement. I hope he had some other savings because, as we all know, Social Security won't be enough to pay his way through a few decades of retirement.

I know this happens across our industry, and I assume it does to others as well. So rather than talk about business valuation, multiples, furniture, fixtures, and equipment (FF&E), EBITDA-Earnings Before Interest Taxes Depreciation and Amortization, and all the other financial terms used in valuing a business, let's focus on the principles that enable us to build a business that can be sold or handed down, providing the owners with the financial security that's deserved for all the years of risk and hard work.

A business is only as valuable as its performance in the owner's absence. If your company requires you to be the driving force at all times, then the company is worth no more than the value of its assets. And let's face it, $45,000 isn't enough for most to fund retirement.

On the flip side, if your company does well regardless of your presence, then you have a company with real value.

Building Real Value—the Key to Firing Yourself

The big question is, How do you put yourself in the position of being able to fire yourself and live comfortably while your business runs itself? Well, obviously that was what all the preceding chapters were meant to reveal. So, let's summarize what's been covered in the previous chapters.

1. *Verify your vision*: Make the vision statement clear enough
    so that everyone understands it, but it's also big enough that
    people around you will want to buy into it with ongoing
    motivation. Remember Martin Holland's very basic
    question, "What do you want?" Why are you considering
    starting a business? What do you hope to get out of such a
    demanding undertaking? If you can't clearly and succinctly
    answer those questions, you're not ready to get started. If
    that's the case, then my advice is to work for someone else
    until you have the answers to those fundamental questions.
    However, if you've already started your business and find
    yourself floundering, then go back and dig deep to answer
    those questions before you write a vision statement. From
    here, follow that statement as your guiding light for every
    decision you face.

2. *Standardize your systems*: As I stated in chapter three,
    standard operating procedures (SOPs) allow you, the
    owner, to be free of the burden of constantly answering
    employees' questions about work procedures. When you
    lack a set of SOPs, you'll find yourself constantly answering
    questions and explaining procedures. Remember, the key
    to good SOPs is to make them specific but simple—and
    keep them up to date.

3. *Choose right and keep it tight*: The teams that win
    championships consist of dedicated and talented—but not
    necessarily all-star level—individuals who know or learn
    how to mesh as a cohesive unit. Be quick to recognize your
    need to hire a new employee, but take your time and do
    your homework as you search for the right person to hire.

Spend the time and money to train the right person, and
people will save you time and money in the long run.

4. *LEAN benefits everyone*: A thriving business cannot rest on
   its laurels. It needs to be always improving, always operating
   in a leaner, more efficient manner. If your business is going
   to survive and thrive, it needs to continually improve,
   eliminate waste, and create value for your customers.
   LEAN has to be a culture, not something employees are
   forced to do. Ultimately, LEAN improves production
   processes, which improves the lives of the employees and
   the owner. And most important, LEAN provides better
   products at better prices to customers.

5. *Update and automate*: A business owner needs to care for
   his or her employees, but even above the employees, he or
   she must care for the customers. Caring for the customers
   means providing them the best possible products or
   services at the lowest possible price. This standard requires
   efficiency, which requires automation and implementation
   of the latest and best technology. Businesses that
   survive and thrive are run by owners who keep up with
   and implement the ever-advancing and ever-evolving
   technological improvements in general and within their
   industry especially.

6. *Train and trust the team*: Keep in mind your primary goal
   is to fire yourself, and to do so you'll need to gradually
   delegate more and more duties to your management staff
   and the rank-and-file employees. If you took to heart the
   advice in step two above, then you have a solid team of
   high-quality employees who can be trained to take on ever

more of the roles you've been performing yourself. If you're not sure you can trust your employees to take on those roles, then you need to reexamine your hiring and training practices.

7. *Your number two needs to be a number one*: Every coach of every good team has one player whom he knows he can count on to call the right plays and make the proper decisions. Your second-in-command is your quarterback, ace pitcher, or point guard on the production line. If your team is well trained and your second-in-command knows your game plan and has the respect of the other team members, then you can sit back and enjoy watching your team rack up win after win.

8. *Expect the unexpected*: No matter how diligent you've been in developing your vision statement and in drafting and coaching your team, sometimes things will just go wrong. Remember Murphy's Law: *"If something can go wrong, it will."* Because you will find yourself facing those inevitable crises, remember these three decrees:

   » Demonstrate humility.

   » Double down on your commitment to your vision statement.

   » Develop a crisis management plan. It's never too soon to prepare for a potential crisis.

9. *Persist, persevere, push through*: Yes, life sometimes serves us a bowl of burned beans rather than ripe, sweet cherries. When those trials hit, sometimes all we can do is persevere or quit. But you're not a quitter, so plan ahead for how you

will stay afloat when the waves are sweeping you toward the rocky reefs. And then hold on tight and keep believing. You will face times when you'll have to choose between the menacing circumstances and your faith in your dream.

10. *Quick responses for quality control*: Customer questions and complaints are keys to quality control. Every time there's a question, it's likely that a flaw is being exposed in the system. That flaw needs to be repaired quickly. If you dismiss customers' questions and complaints as cranks wasting your time, you'll soon find your business being overtaken by your competitors who quickly responded to those customers.

11. *Service sells*: I'm convinced that the best way to do business is to see my customers as friends for whom I provide a service. If you focus most or all your attention on sales with little to no regard for service after the sale, before long you'll be losing more customers out the back door than you gain through the front door. Although that after-the-sale service isn't cheap, it's necessary. Remember, satisfied customers can be your best advertisers, and dissatisfied customers can be your worst ones.

12. *Pitch the product; pitch the story*: Some products are so appealing, so tempting at an elemental level that they sell themselves. Remember the irresistible five-dollar donuts? We do well if we can create such appealing products. But most products are not that inspiring. More often, we need to sell the story. To do that we need to *build the personal foundation*. And to build the personal foundation, we need personal awareness, customer awareness, and product

awareness. If I know who I am, the customers' story, and what my products are (their stories), I can pitch "the story."

13. *What do you want?* Ah, yes, inflection often identifies intent. In this case, the inflection is calm, simply inquiring about one's goal. *What are your life's priorities?* Your priorities will drive your goals. As a businessperson, one of your top priorities is to increase sales. One of the best ways to do that is to follow the sales funnel and set sales goals accordingly.

14. *Educating, equipping, and empowering:* Generally, customers buy from companies or individuals they feel they know and can trust. To develop that sense of familiarity and dependability, you need to get your story out to the buying public. Doing that sets you on the path to inbound marketing, which is sometimes described as the magnet method. On the other hand, outbound marketing is often described as the megaphone method. The megaphone method shouts your message out to anyone who might be within earshot, while you hope some of those whom the message reached might respond. The magnet method is more subtle and targeted, as it draws those targeted people in. Modern technology facilitates the inbound marketing method. Ask yourself, Is your business set up to use technological advances as a means of inbound marketing?

15. *You really don't want ignorant employees:* It isn't just you and your customers who need to be educated. Your employees will benefit from a bit of education about the company's economic situation. And when employees gain a benefit from the company, they usually return a benefit

to the company. What are some benefits of this employee knowledge?

» It instills a sense of pride of accomplishment (personal and team).

» It helps build team unity, which benefits the entire team.

» It helps each team member understand that the owner is their ally, not their foe.

» It can improve employee retention.

16. *A thirsty optimist will drink half a glass*: Optimism and realism are not mutually exclusive. In chapter eight, I warned of the need to be prepared for life's inevitable crises. Life on this planet is not perfect. But let's be honest—for most human beings, the good times outweigh the bad. The person who refuses to believe that fact is the one who is ignoring reality. And that person should not seek a career in sales. When you, your new salesperson, or your entire skilled sales team hits the road, dials the phone, or sends that promotional mailing, do so with a mindset of abundance rather than of scarcity.

17. *Turn away toxic team members*: Dismissing an employee is never easy. But often, failing to do so can destroy a business. Preserving a positive company culture guided by a strong mission statement is too important to let a destructive employee poison it. Before firing any employee, first the owner should be certain he or she didn't contribute to the employee's poor performance by not providing proper orientation and training. But as soon as it's clear

that the employee is a bad fit because of his or her own shortcomings, then the owner should not waste time in doing what must be done. And then do it by the book.

Well, that's it, folks. I hope you enjoyed and took to heart the advice provided in this book—particularly if you're seriously contemplating starting a small business. If you have feedback for me on this book, please send it. You can contact me on my company website or through my blog or podcast. You can also contact me through any of those methods if you'd like to schedule me to speak to your group about business ideas.

Now, go out there and prepare for that day when *you will fire yourself!*

COMPREHENSIVE LIST OF REFERENCE WEBSITES

Ongoing training: A well-trained employee is more likely to be a productive and contented employee. For more assistance, see "The 8 Best Training Methods for Your Employees."[123]

Good communication: An employee who understands company objectives and expectations is also more likely to be a productive and contented employee. For more assistance on company communication, see "5 Proven Ways to Improve Your Company's Communication."[124]

Performance reviews: Employees need to know, ongoing, what they're doing well and where they need to improve. And, of course, pay raises should be tied to good performance. For more assistance on performance reviews, see "10 Key Tips for Effective Employee Performance Reviews."[125]

Positive work environment: Employees who are free from harassment, who feel they are part of a dedicated and valued team, and who feel respected are more likely to perform at high levels. For more assistance on creating a positive work environment, see "10 Ways to Create a Positive Business Environment."[126]

Online advice on establishing a profit-sharing plan for your business that incentivizes business growth:

- "Profit Sharing Plans for Small Businesses"[127]
- "How to Create a Profit-Sharing Plan"[128]
- "3 Approaches to Profit Sharing"[129]

Website offering guidance in creating your CMP:

- "Elements of an Effective Crisis Management Plan"[130]

Website-building references:

- "10 Top Website Design Services"[131]
- "7 Simple Steps to Create a Website for Your Small Business"[132]

Miscellaneous:

- "4 Things All Employees Should Know about Financial Analysis"[133]
- "Ten Rules for Great Finance"[134]
- "8 Ways to Become an Optimist"[135]
- "3 Ways to Achieve a Winning Sales Attitude"[136]
- "How Much Is a Typical Retainer Fee for a Lawyer?"[137]
- *Employment Law Handbook*
- "How to Terminate an Employee (with Sample Scripts)"[138]
- "Guide To Severance Pay"[139]

ENDNOTES

1   B. C. Forbes, *Forbes Epigrams: A Thousand Thoughts on Life and Business* (New York: B. C. Forbes Publishing Company, 1922).

2   "Passion in the Workplace with Bobby Lewis," The Push Thru podcast, January 30, 2018.

3   "1978 Albertson's Supermarket Commercial (David Ruprecht)," YouTube video, uploaded May 20, 2016, https://www.youtube.com/watch?v=udik1t-gahE.

4   Terri Guillemets, "For Good or for Bad," Inkpots & Daydreams, October 12, 2005, https://www.terriguillemets.com/2005-10-12-once-lighthouse-seen-rest-sea-ignored/.

5   Sean Peek, "What Is a Vision Statement?," Business News Daily, updated May 7, 2020, https://www.businessnewsdaily.com/3882-vision-statement.html.

6   Joseph Folkman, "8 Ways to Ensure Your Vision Is Valued," *Forbes*, April 22, 2014, https://www.forbes.com/sites/joefolkman/2014/04/22/8-ways-to-ensure-your-vision-is-valued/?sh=180c2e664524.

7   Daniel W. Rasmus, "Defining Your Company's Vision," *Fast Company*, February 28, 2012, https://www.fastcompany.com/1821021/defining-your-companys-vision.

8   "IKEA Vision, Culture and Values," IKEA, ac-

cessed July 7, 2021, https://ikea.jobs.cz/en/vision-cul-ture-and-values/.

9	"About," Microsoft, accessed July 7, 2021, https://www.microsoft.com/en-us/about.

10	Bart Dohmen, "Vision Statements: Why Crush Adidas Is Essential for the Attractions Market," Blooloop, April 27, 2020, https://blooloop.com/brands-ip/opinion/vision-statement-attractions-crush-adidas/.

11	"Walmart.com's History and Mission," Walmart, accessed July 7, 2021, https://www.walmart.com/help/article/walmart-com-s-history-and-mission/a62ce500758c4746a211d00d7c2acfcd.

12	Saji Ijiyemi (@sajigroup), Twitter, November 5, 2015, 9:24 a.m., https://twitter.com/sajigroup/status/662274200607072256.

13	"Bill Romanoswki," NFL, accessed July 7, 2021, https://www.nfl.com/players/bill-romanowski/stats/career.

14	"Dirtiest Professional Team Players," ESPN, accessed July 7, 2021, https://www.espn.com/page2/s/list/dirtiest/players.html.

15	Forbes, *Forbes Epigrams* (1922).

16	Merriam-Webster, "standard operating proce-dure," accessed July 7, 2021, https://www.merriam-webster.com/dictionary/standard%20operating%20procedure.

17	Michael Jordan, *I Can't Accept Not Trying: Michael Jordan on the Pursuit of Excellence* (San Francisco: Harper San Francisco, 1994).

18	Chris Haney, "On This Day: Michael Jordan's Last Game Was Played 18 Years Ago," Outsider, April 16, 2021, https://outsider.com/news/sports/on-this-day-michael-jordan-last-game-played-18-years-ago/.

19	Barnaby Lane, "Michael Jordan's Ruthlessness

Why He's GOAT Over LeBron James," Insider, December 14, 2020, https://www.insider.com/michael-jordans-ruthlessness-why-goat-over-lebron-james-ex-team-mate-2020-12.

20   Eddie Bitar, "5 Reasons Why Michael Jordan Is the GOAT," Fadeaway World, February 17, 2021, https://fadeawayworld.net/nba/5-reasons-why-michael-jordan-is-the-goat.

21   Bitar, "5 Reasons."

22   Jordan, *I Can't Accept Not Trying.*

23   Thomas J. Brown, Jr., "October 16, 1969: Miracle Mets Become First Expansion Team to Win World Series," Society for American Baseball Research, 2018, https://sabr.org/gamesproj/game/october-16-1969-miracle-mets-become-first-expansion-team-to-win-a-world-series/.

24   "1969 Baltimore Orioles Roster," Baseball Almanac, accessed July 7, 2021, https://www.baseball-almanac.com/teamstats/roster.php?y=1969&t=BAL.

25   "12 Funny Factoids about the 198 Players Drafted Ahead of Tom Brady in 2000," Fox Sports, February 22, 2016, https://www.foxsports.com/stories/nfl/12-funny-factoids-about-the-198-players-drafted-ahead-of-tom-brady-in-2000.

26   Neil Pane, "All the Ways That Tom Brady Is Football's GOAT," FiveThirtyEight, February 9, 2021, https://fivethirtyeight.com/features/all-the-ways-that-tom-brady-is-footballs-goat/.

27   "Trail Blazers Told Bulls They'd Draft Sam Bowie over Michael Jordan a Month Early," NBC Sports, April 22, 2020, https://www.nbcsports.com/chicago/bulls/trail-blazers-told-bulls-theyd-draft-sam-bowie-over-michael-jordan-month-early.

28   Bryant Knox, "Remembering Why the Portland

Trail Blazers Chose Greg Oden over Kevin Durant," Bleacher Report, May 22, 2012, https://bleacherreport. com/articles/1188523-remembering-why-the-portland-trail-blazers-chose-greg-oden-over-kevin-durant.

29   Joe Kozlowski, "Packers Quarterback Matt Flynn Turned 7 NFL Starts into a $19 Million Career," Sports-casting, April 30, 2020, https://www.sportscasting.com/ packers-quarterback-matt-flynn-turned-7-nfl-starts-into-a-19-million-career/.

30   Mookie Alexander, "Super Bowl 48 Flashback: The Seahawks Defense Was Great, but So Was Russell Wilson," SB Nation Field Gulls, February 3, 2017, https:// www.fieldgulls.com/2017/2/3/14476488/super-bowl-xl-viii-flashback-seattle-seahawks-vs-denver-broncos-rus-sell-wilson.

31   F. John Reh, "The Cost of High Employee Turn-over," The Balance Careers, updated August 13, 2019, https://www.thebalancecareers.com/the-high-cost-of-high-employee-turnover-2276010.

32   "The Real Cost of Employee Turnover in 2020," TERRA Staffing Group, November 4, 2020, https://www. terrastaffinggroup.com/resources/blog/cost-of-employ-ee-turnover/.

33   Ronald Blum, "Curt Flood Set Off the Base-ball Free-Agent Revolution 50 Years Ago," Denver Post, updated December 24, 2019, https://www.denverpost. com/2019/12/24/curt-flood-mlb-free-agent-revolution/.

34   "How to Create an Effective New Employee Ori-entation Program," Indeed, March 24, 2021, https://www. indeed.com/career-advice/career-development/new-em-ployee-orientation-program.

35   Susan M. Heathfield, "What's in a Comprehen-sive Employee Benefits Package?" The Balance Careers, updated November 20, 2019, https://www.thebalanceca-

reers.com/what-s-in-a-comprehensive-employee-bene-
fits-package-1917860.

36   Murray Newlands, "5 Proven Ways to Improve Your Company's Communication," *Forbes*,
January 26, 2016, https://www.forbes.com/sites/
mnewlands/2016/01/26/5-proven-ways-to-improve-your-
companys-communication/?sh=1293cdf23118.

37   Ahmad Emarah, "Top 10 Ways to Create a Positive Work Environment," LinkedIn, December 31, 2020,
https://www.linkedin.com/pulse/top-10-ways-create-pos-
itive-work-environment-ahmad-emarah/.

38   "How to Calculate Employee Turnover Rate,"
Indeed, March 26, 2021, https://www.indeed.com/ca-
reer-advice/career-development/how-to-calculate-turn-
over-rate.

39   Paul A. Akers, *2 Second Lean: How to Grow People and Build a Lean Culture* (Bellingham, WA: FastCap,
2011).

40   "What Is Lean?" Lean Enterprise Institute (LEP),
accessed July 7, 2021, https://www.lean.org/WhatsLean/.

41   Akers, *2 Second Lean.*

42   Akers, *2 Second Lean.*

43   "What is Lean?" LEP.

44   Clara Shih, "The Rise of Millennials, Crowd-
sourcing, and Automation Are Going to Reshape the
World," *Fast Company*, February 3, 2016, https://www.
fastcompany.com/3055899/the-rise-of-millennials-
crowdsourcing-and-automation-are-going-to-reshape-
the-world.

45   Mark Cuban (@mcuban), Twitter, February 19, 2017, https://twitter.com/mcuban/sta-
tus/833476263339814913.

46   "Cars in the 1920s—The Early Automobile Industry," World History, August 8, 2017, https://worldhistory.

us/american-history/cars-in-the-1920s-the-early-auto-mobile-industry.php.

47   "Cars in the 1920s," World History.

48   Allen Finn, "35 Face-Melting Email Marketing Stats," WordStream, updated November 1, 2020, https://www.wordstream.com/blog/ws/2017/06/29/email-marketing-statistics.

49   Gadjo Sevilla, "The Best Email Marketing Software for 2020," PC Magazine, updated June 24, 2021, https://www.pcmag.com/picks/the-best-email-marketing-software.

50   Arthur Zuckerman, "40 Direct Mail Statistics: 2020/2021 Behavior, Trends & Data Analysis," CompareCamp, May 11, 2020, https://comparecamp.com/direct-mail-statistics/.

51   "6 Key Benefits of Using Payroll Software for Small Businesses," QuickBooks, January 6, 2021, https://quickbooks.intuit.com/uk/blog/benefits-of-payroll-software/.

52   Charlette Beasley, "6 Best Free Payroll Software for 2021," Fit Small Business, January 8, 2021, https://fitsmallbusiness.com/free-payroll-software/.

53   Anna Johansson, "The 'Whys' of Why You Should Consider HR Software for Your Small Business," Entrepreneur, March 20, 2017, https://www.entrepreneur.com/article/290771/.

54   "Supply Chain Management Software for Small Businesses," Kabbage Resource Center, accessed September 18, 2021, https://www.kabbage.com/resource-center/manage/supply-chain-management-software-for-small-businesses/.

55   Lars Lofgren, "Best Supply Chain Management Software," Quick Sprout, December 28, 2020, https://www.quicksprout.com/best-supply-chain-manage-

ment-software/.

56   "Six Advantages of Expense Management App for Small Businesses," Expense OnDemand, February 10, 2021, https://www.expenseondemand.com/6-advantages-of-expense-management-app-for-small-businesses.

57   "Cover Story Reagan on Decision-Making, Planning, Gorbachev, and More," CNN Money, originally in *Fortune* magazine, September 15, 1986, https://money.cnn.com/magazines/fortune/fortune_archive/1986/09/15/68051/index.htm.

58   "From George Washington to Lieutenant Colonel Joseph Reed, 23 January 1776," National Archives, January 23, 1776, accessed July 8, 2021, https://founders.archives.gov/documents/Washington/03-03-02-0123.

59   "General Charles Lee," Revolutionary War, updated March 4, 2020, https://www.revolutionary-war.net/general-charles-lee/.

60   Peter Kozodoy, "Hiring a Second-In-Command? This Former Executive Says Don't Do This," *Inc.*, July 7, 2017, https://www.inc.com/peter-kozodoy/how-to-hire-a-brilliant-executive-according-to-the.html.

61   "Profit Sharing Plans for Small Businesses," U.S. Department of Labor, accessed August 11, 2021, https://www.dol.gov/agencies/ebsa/about-ebsa/our-activities/resource-center/publications/profitsharingplansforsmallbusinesses.

62   Eric Carter, "How to Create a Profit Sharing Plan for Your Business," QuickBooks, June 14, 2017, https://quickbooks.intuit.com/r/business-planning/create-profit-sharing-plan-business/.

63   Stephen Bruce, "The 3 Approaches to Profit-Sharing," HR Daily Advisor, April 30, 2014, https://hrdailyadvisor.blr.com/2014/04/30/the-3-approaches-to-profit-sharing/.

64   "Elements of an Effective Crisis Management Plan," Centre Technologies, June 10, 2015, https://www.insider.com/michael-jordans-ruthlessness-why-goat-over-lebron-james-ex-teammate-2020-12.
65   Hayley Jennings, "7 Essential Elements of a Crisis Plan," PR News, September 24, 2018, https://www.prnewsonline.com/essential-crisis-plan-elements.
66   "Office Jokes: Laugh Out Loud with These Funny Office Jokes," Reader's Digest, accessed July 8, 2021, https://www.rd.com/jokes/office/.
67   H. G. Wells, You Can't Be Too Careful (H. G. Wells Library, 2016), 177.
68   Debra Michals, ed., "Harriet Tubman," National Women's History Museum, accessed July 8, 2021, https://www.womenshistory.org/education-resources/biographies/harriet-tubman.
69   Kate Clifford Larson, "Harriet Tubman Biography," Harriet Tubman Biography, accessed July 8, 2021, http://www.harriettubmanbiography.com/harriet-tubman-biography.html.
70   Larson, "Harriet Tubman Biography."
71   Barbara Maranzani, "Harriet Tubman: 8 Facts about the Daring Abolitionist," History, updated January 25, 2021, https://www.history.com/news/harriet-tubman-facts-daring-raid.
72   Michals, "Harriet Tubman."
73   Leonard DeGraaf, Edison and the Rise of Innovation (New York: Sterling Signature, 2013).
74   Frank Lewis Dyer and Thomas Commerford Martin, Edison: His Life and Inventions (New York: Harpers, 1929), 616.
75   Will Durant, The Story of Philosophy: The Lives and Opinions of the World's Greatest Philosophers (New York: Pocket Books, 1991).

76   Houston Mitchell, "Yogi Berra Dies at 90: Here Are Some of His Greatest Quotes," *Los Angeles Times*, May 12, 2015, https://www.latimes.com/sports/sportsnow/la-sp-sn-yogi-berra-turns-90-quotes-20150512-story.html.

77   *Jerry Maguire*, directed by Cameron Crowe, (Sony Pictures Releasing, 1996), DVD, 139 mins.

78   Crystal Raypole, "A Beginner's Guide to Reading Body Language," Healthline, January 15, 2020, https://www.healthline.com/health/body-language.

79   *Jerry Maguire*, dir. Cameron Crowe.

80   Emma Martins, "Why Excellent Customer Service Is Crucial to Improving Sales," FM Outsource, March 18, 2021, https://fmoutsource.com/resources/how-customer-service-affects-sales/.

81   David Oglivy, *Confessions of an Advertising Man* (London: Southbank Publishing, 2012).

82   "How to Market on a Low Budget: Part 1 with Khalil Benalioulhaj," The Push Thru podcast, February 26, 2018.

83   Ibid.

84   Ibid.

85   Ibid.

86   Ibid.

87   Ibid.

88   Ibid.

89   Ibid.

90   Lars Lofgren, "Best Web Design Services," Quick Sprout, June 25, 2021, https://www.quicksprout.com/best-web-design-services/.

91   Rose Wheeler, "7 Simple Steps to Create a Website for Your Small Business," The Blueprint, updated February 1, 2021, https://www.fool.com/the-blueprint/how-to-make-a-website/.

92   Adrian Swinscoe, "The Best Marketing Doesn't Feel Like Marketing—Interview with Tom Fishburne," Customer Think, October 25, 2017, https://customerthink.com/the-best-marketing-doesnt-feel-like-marketing-interview-with-tom-fishburne/.

93   "How to Market on a Low Budget."

94   Ibid.

95   Ibid.

96   Ibid.

97   Ibid.

98   Amanda Sellers, "What Is the Buyer's Journey?" HubSpot, updated May 12, 2021, https://blog.hubspot.com/sales/what-is-the-buyers-journey.

99   Benjamin Brewster, "Theory and Practice," *Yale Literary Magazine*, February 1882, https://books.google.com/

100   Jack Stack, *The Great Game of Business: The Only Sensible Way to Run a Company* (New York: Currency, 2013).

101   Yogi Berra, *The Yogi Book: I Really Didn't Say Everything I Said I Did!* (New York: Workman Publishing, 1998).

102   "4 Things All Employees Should Know about Financial Analysis," Andromeda Simulations International, accessed July 8, 2021, https://income-outcome.com/financial-analysis/.

103   Ari Weinzweig, "Ten Rules for Great Finance," ZingTrain, accessed July 8, 2021, https://www.zingtrain.com/article/ten-rules-for-great-finance/.

104   Berra, *The Yogi Book* (1998).

105   Berra, *The Yogi Book* (1998).

106   "Efficient Desalination of Seawater," Keiken, accessed July 8, 2021, https://www.keiken-engineering.com/en/reverse-osmosis-one-of-the-best-methods-for-ef-

ficient-desalination-of-seawater/.

107   "The World's 3 Trillion Trees, Mapped," the *Washington Post*, September 16, 2015, https://www.washingtonpost.com/news/energy-environment/wp/2015/09/16/the-countries-of-the-world-ranked-by-their-tree-wealth/.

108   "Current World Population," Worldometer, accessed July 8, 2021, https://www.worldometers.info/world-population/.

109   "How Much Lumber in That Tree?" Michigan State University, November 16, 2015, https://www.canr.msu.edu/resources/how_much_lumber_in_that_tree_e2915.

110   "U.S. and World Population Clock," U.S. Census Bureau, accessed July 8, 2021, https://www.census.gov/popclock/.

111   Colleen Stanley, "3 Ways to Achieve a Winning Sales Attitude," HubSpot, updated December 8, 2017, https://blog.hubspot.com/sales/sales-attitude.

112   Paul Strack, "The Two Travelers," LinkedIn, April 3, 2020, https://www.linkedin.com/pulse/two-travelers-paul-strack/.

113   Martin Seligman, *Learned Optimism: How to Change Your Mind and Your Life* (New York: Vintage, 2006).

114   Deborah Kotz and Angela Haupt, "8 Ways to Become an Optimist," U.S. News & World Report, March 26, 2012, https://health.usnews.com/health-news/living-well-usn/slideshows/8-ways-to-become-an-optimist?slide=2.

115   Liz Gannes, "Charlie Ergen on Dish's Company Culture: It's Not That We're Mean, It's That We're Like an Indiana Jones Movie," All Things D, February 11, 2013, http://allthingsd.com/20130211/charlie-ergen-on-dishs-company-culture-its-not-that-were-mean-its-that-were-like-an-indiana-jones-movie/.

116 "The Real Cost of Employee Turnover," TERRA.

117 Ivan Wylda, "How Much Is a Typical Retainer Fee for a Lawyer?" Biz Epic, October 2, 2019, https://www.bizepic.com/2019/10/02/how-much-is-a-typical-retainer-fee-for-a-lawyer/.

118 Riia O'Donnell, "How to Terminate an Employee (with Sample Scripts)," Workest, October 2, 2019, https://www.zenefits.com/workest/what-to-say-when-terminating-an-employee-with-sample-scripts/.

119 "Severance Pay," US Department of Labor, accessed July 8, 2021, https://www.dol.gov/general/topic/wages/severancepay.

120 "Oklahoma—Minimum Wage, Overtime, Hours, and Leave," Employment Law Handbook, accessed July 8, 2021, https://www.employmentlawhandbook.com/wage-and-hour-laws/state-wage-and-hour-laws/oklahoma/#9.

121 "Guide to Severance Pay," Indeed, February 9, 2021, https://www.indeed.com/career-advice/pay-salary/guide-to-severance-pay.

122 "Guide to Severance Pay for Fired Employees," Indeed, February 22, 2021, https://www.indeed.com/career-advice/career-development/fired-severance.

123 "The 8 Best Types of Training Methods for Your Employees," Indeed, February 22, 2021, https://www.indeed.com/career-advice/career-development/best-types-employee-training-methods.

124 Murray Newlands, "5 Proven Ways To Improve Your Company's Communication," *Forbes*, January 26, 2016, https://www.forbes.com/sites/mnewlands/2016/01/26/5-proven-ways-to-improve-your-companys-communication/?sh=5df-90cc43118.

125 Susan M. Heathfield, "10 key Tips for Effective Employee Performance Reviews," The Balance Careers,

updated February 19, 2021, https://www.thebalanceca-reers.com/effective-performance-review-tips-1918842.

126   Ahmad Emarah, "Top 10 Ways to Create a Positive Work Environment," LinkedIn, December 31, 2020, https://www.linkedin.com/pulse/top-10-ways-create-pos-itive-work-environment-ahmad-emarah/.

127   "Profit Sharing Plans for Small Businesses," U.S. Department of Labor.

128   Carter, "How to Create a Profit-Sharing Plan for Your Business."

129   Bruce, "The 3 Approaches to Profit-Sharing."

130   "Elements of an Effective Crisis Management Plan," Centre Technologies.

131   Lofgren, "Best Web Design Services."

132   Wheeler, "7 Simple Steps to Create a Website for Your Small Business."

133   "4 Things All Employees Should Know about Financial Analysis," Andromeda Simulations.

134   Weinzweig, "Ten Rules for Great Finance."

135   Deborah Kotz and Angela Haupt, "8 Ways to Become an Optimist."

136   Stanley, "3 Ways to Achieve a Winning Sales Attitude."

137   Wylda, "How Much Is a Typical Retainer Fee for a Lawyer?"

138   O'Donnell, "How to Terminate an Employee (with Sample Scripts)."

139   "Guide to Severance Pay," Indeed.

Made in the USA
Monee, IL
05 February 2022

90764049R00111